GIRLS RULE!

GIRLS RULE!

The Glory

and Spirit

of *Women*

in *Sports*

Foreword by Billie Jean King

Written by Ken Rappoport & Barry Wilner

**Andrews McMeel
Publishing**

Kansas City

Girls Rule! The Glory and Spirit of Women in Sports
By Ken Rappoport and Barry Wilner
© 2000 Design and Compilation Lionheart Books, Ltd.

Girls Rule! The Glory and Spirit of Women in Sports
was produced by Lionheart Books, Ltd.,
5105 Peachtree Industrial Boulevard, Atlanta, Georgia 30341

Design: Carley Wilson Brown

ISBN: 0-7407-1171-7

Library of Congress Cataloging-in-Publication Data on file

For Bernice, my noon, my midnight, my talk, my song.

—*K.R.*

To my wife Helene, son Evan, and the three girls who rule: Nicole, Jamie, and Tricia.

—*B.W.*

By Billie Jean King

*d*efining moments.

As I watched the U.S. soccer team win the World Cup last summer, it struck me that this victory was but one of the many defining moments in women's sports in the 20th century. What truly amazed me was how frequent they have become.

In looking back at 1926 and Gertrude Ederle, who was determined to become the first woman to swim the English Channel. Against great odds, not to mention the strong, unpredictable currents, the undaunted Ederle made two attempts. The first time, she failed. On the second, she succeeded.

And so it was with many of the women in *Girls Rule!* All of them, in a manner of speaking, had to swim against the tide in order to prove themselves as both athletes and women. Like Ederle, they faced their own challenges, their own demons, and they conquered them all.

I know what they went through, because I did it too. And I'm proud that the success I achieved on the tennis court served as a platform from which I could promote equality and elevate the status of women in sports.

Of course, Title IX helped immeasurably. But even before this historic legislation was passed in 1972, there were inspirational stories such as Ederle's to shed light on the dark ages of women's athletics.

One such story was that of Babe Didrikson Zaharias, who, because she was adept at a wide variety of sports, practically became a movement unto herself.

Not only was she an Olympic track and field champion, a standout on the basketball court and the golf course, Babe was partly responsible for the establishment of the LPGA. Her achievements during the first half of the century stand as some of the greatest in women's sports history.

Then there was Sonja Henie, whose career laid the foundation for future generations of women on ice. After she completely revolutionized the sport of figure skating, she went to Hollywood and became one of its biggest stars, making her an entertainment icon on two continents; one who brought unprecedented attention to her sport and the women in it. Consequently, figure skating is the one sport where women have always been the main attraction.

Another inspiration was Wilma Rudolph, who, through her unwavering perseverance, overcame poverty and polio to become an Olympic champion and then a crusader for human rights. Then, too, there was Donna de Varona, an Olympic swimming gold medalist who would pioneer the role of women in sports broadcasting before becoming a leader of the movement for gender equality in athletics.

These are merely a few of the women whose achievements are chronicled in this book, women who won championships as they battled for equality long before federal legislation helped them to achieve it.

When I look back on my career, which began in the early 1960s, I see just how far women's sports have

come. But I also see how much farther we have to go, though this in no way discounts the tremendous strides that have been made in the acceptance of women athletes. Modern tennis is celebrated as much by the achievements of Martina Hingis, Lindsay Davenport, and Venus or Serena Williams as it is by any of the men on the circuit. And the same holds true for other sports as well. For every Michael Johnson, there is a Gail Devers. For every Dan Jansen, there is a Bonnie Blair. As important as Arnold Palmer was to men's golf, Nancy Lopez has been just as big a force on the women's tour.

The horizon is equally bright in team competition. The WNBA has been a wonderful success story. The

"When I look back on my career, which began in the early 1960s, I see just how far women's sports have come. But I also see how much farther we have to go, though this in no way discounts the tremendous strides that have been made in the acceptance of women athletes."

women's NCAA basketball tournament has become a major event on the calendar. A professional fast-pitch softball league exists, and women's hockey is beginning to receive more recognition.

As for soccer, well, who was selected as 1999's Team of the Year? Who are the most famous and popular soccer players in America? Why, they're so famous they're even known by their first names: Mia, Brandi, and Briana.

But this isn't just a book about women athletes. It's a book about goals and dreams. It's a book about humanity.

In *Girls Rule!* we read the uplifting stories of skaters like Peggy Fleming and Nancy Kerrigan and marvel at the versatility of track stars like Jackie Joyner-Kersee and Fanny Blankers-Koen, the courtside brilliance of basketball's Jennifer Gillom, and the indefatigable spirit of Shirley Muldowney. And we look back at the 1996 Atlanta Games which, because of the superlative performances recorded there, became known as the Women's Olympics.

Then there are intense rivalries and enduring friendships like the one between Chris Evert and Martina Navratilova. We read of the courage Rudolph and Devers demonstrated in overcoming disease. We witness the fortitude shown by Janet Guthrie and Julie Krone as they pioneered the way for women in what were traditionally considered to be men's sports.

As we reached the new millennium, so much had changed for women athletes that I had to smile.

Back in 1971 or 1972, before I played Mr. Riggs, women were playing for less than $1 million on the tennis tour. The disparity between the fees men received and those which were awarded to women had become so great that we had to make threats not to participate at tour stops before our demands for increased prize money were taken seriously. Now, thanks to the unwavering conviction of a few, there is more than $50 million in prize money on the women's tour.

For me, though, it was always about social change and helping to move us forward. It wasn't just about sports, it was about women and men and how we treat each other.

I knew when I played Bobby Riggs in 1973 that I was representing women's sports in general and not merely those women who played professional tennis. That match was about such things as self-esteem and allowing girls to

Venus Williams *(left)* **gets a high-five from U.S. captain Billie Jean King during the finals of the Fed Cup in Stanford, C.A., 1999.**

have their dreams. In those days, women were not truly accepted as athletes. That's why I accepted the challenge, so that girls and women could feel positive about participating in athletics. There should be nothing to stop them from pursuing and fulfilling their dreams.

The Women's Sports Foundation has played a critical role in advancing those goals. By having such intelligent, persuasive, and driven people as Donna de Varona, Donna Lopiano, Nancy Lieberman-Cline, and Julie Foudy, to name a few, heading the organization, it has made a significant impact on sports and society. Founding the Women's Sports Foundation stands as one of my proudest achievements.

I foresee that the next few years will bring a greater participation in coed sports. In that regard, World Team Tennis has been a trendsetter as an equal opportunity team sport. Should others choose to follow this example and extend parity to members of both sexes, then I will be even more grateful to have established

World Team Tennis and to have watched its influence spread to other sports.

In words and pictures that capture the glory and spirit of women in sports, *Girls Rule!* tells the stories of champions who have left a legacy of triumph in the face of adversity. From the early 20th century, when Madge Syers was forced to compete against men in figure skating, to Brandi Chastain's exclamation point on the greatest tournament in the history of women's sports, the stories are powerful and poignant, as energizing as they are enlightening.

I'm proud to have played a role in that history, and I hope to continue watching more of these defining moments for a long time to come.

May 2000
Billie Jean King
Chicago, Illinois

NO PERSON IN THE UNITED STATES SHALL, ON THE BASIS OF SEX, BE
EXCLUDED FROM PARTICIPATION IN, BE DENIED THE BENEFITS OF,
OR BE SUBJECTED TO DISCRIMINATION UNDER ANY EDUCATIONAL
PROGRAM OR ACTIVITY RECEIVING FEDERAL FINANCIAL ASSISTANCE.

—*Title IX of the Education Amendments Act of 1972*

---

*W*hen Brandi Chastain went shirtless in Pasadena, she caused quite a sensation. Her victory celebration did more than attract the media, it also drew attention to the benefits American female athletes had reaped from Title IX legislation.

Dubbed the "Title IX Babies," Chastain and her teammates on the World Cup champion United States soccer team were representative of the dramatic growth of women's sports in America during the latter part of the 20th century. And it was all thanks to federal legislation which mandated equal funding for men's and women's sports.

When Title IX was passed into law in 1972 as part of the Education Amendments Act, it included all aspects of educational programs in America. However, the effect it had on women's sports was by far the most visible.

Before Title IX was passed into law, only one in twenty-seven girls played organized sports in high school. In the 1990s, it was one of three. In 1972, the average number of women's sports teams at colleges was 2.1 per school. In 1999, the number was 7.7. Women's participation in college sports tripled from 31,000 in the 1970s to 110,000 in the 1990s. In 1972, less than $100,000 was spent on athletic scholarships for women in America. By the mid-'90s, it was close to $180 million.

And women weren't just putting their stamps on the traditional sports of tennis and golf. It was a sign of the times that, in 1997, the athletic director at Michigan State cut men's lacrosse while adding women's fencing. In Florida high schools, women's sports featured everything from flag football to field hockey. And in Iowa, as in many other states across the nation, girls high school basketball was never more popular.

Title IX had a difficult path to follow before it became law. The legislation met opposition from many schools who feared that Title IX would divert funds from big money-making sports such as football and basketball. The National Collegiate Athletic Association (NCAA) sued to have the legislation declared illegal. The suit failed, as did attempts by lawmakers to diminish the legislation's impact.

Things today are still far from perfect. Women's groups complain that Title IX has been loosely enforced, that many schools aren't in compliance with

Olympic athlete Jackie Joyner-Kersee speaks in the Old Executive Office Building in Washington in 1997 during a ceremony to celebrate the 25th anniversary of Title IX, which prohibits sex discrimination in federally assisted education programs.

the law, and that women still lag behind men in the sports funding department. Some feel it will still take ten or twelve years for women to achieve parity.

Nevertheless, America's national women's teams reaped the benefit of Title IX at the 1996 Olympics. The United States had 277 women competing in Atlanta, the most female participants ever at the Games. The U.S. women won gold medals in soccer, softball, and basketball.

"Programs had to be built from scratch when Title IX was passed, and it's taken [until the '90s] for it to really show," said Tiffeny Milbrett, a forward who played soccer at the University of Portland before joining the U.S. Olympic and World Cup teams. "There are many countries where the women don't have the opportunities we've had, and might never get them. So Title IX is a major reason the U.S. is able to compete [internationally] and do well on the highest levels."

The Title IX story is still being told as it continues to open doors, knock down barriers, and help women to eliminate stereotypes in sports.

chapter one

"We've always said we're America's best-kept secret," Foudy said with a chuckle. "Looks like the secret is out."

Soccer Mamas

Silence. Utter silence.

After more than two hours of screams, chants, cheers and groans, the Rose Bowl fell silent. For two full halves and two overtime periods, noise echoed throughout the San Gabriel Mountains. The ebb and flow that defines the beauty of soccer had come to this: a penalty-kick shootout between the United States and China for the world title.

A crowd of 90,185, the largest ever to witness a women's sporting event, held its breath as Brandi Chastain walked to the penalty spot for a shot that would decide the championship. Millions of fans throughout America had already been captivated by these women, this team, and the tournament. Rarely had any sports competition—and certainly none involving either soccer or women—turned into such a national phenomenon.

Chastain wasn't thinking about any of that as she prepared to challenge China's renowned goalkeeper, Gao Hong. If she had been, Chastain would have been looking back at the most incredible ride imaginable.

The U.S. team that gathered in central New Jersey before its World Cup opener was no novice to the

U.S. forward Mia Hamm *(right)* dribbles the ball past China's midfielder Wang Liping at Giants Stadium in East Rutherford, N.J., April 25, 1999.

spotlight or to the pressures of international competition. Eight years earlier, an American squad had gone to China and won the first Women's World Cup.

"Yeah," recalled Julie Foudy, co-captain of the 1999 team and a key member of the '91 champions, "there was one reporter at the airport to ask us about it when we got home."

There weren't many more on hand for the early training sessions leading up to the first game, against Denmark, at Giants Stadium. Why should there be? Sure, this team had won the 1996 Olympic crown in dramatic fashion, beating China 2-1 before 76,000 fans.

There were indications that both this team and this event were something special. Mia Hamm, the world's best player, was already a star—she had even appeared in Gatorade commercials with Michael Jordan. David Letterman had adopted the U.S. squad, featuring "Soccer Mamas" regularly on his television show.

On July 10, 1999, at the Rose Bowl in Pasadena, California, a crowd of 90,185, the largest ever to witness a women's sporting event,

held its breath as Brandi Chastain scored the winning penalty kick against China's goalkeeper, Gao Hong.

Still, it was soccer—Women's soccer.

"This is what we have been waiting for, the moment for people to start watching us and for us to get more fans each and every day. This can be our breakthrough," Kristine Lilly said.

Then Lilly looked around and saw perhaps a dozen fans and even fewer media members at the Pingry School, where the team practiced.

"It's difficult," she admitted. "We went to the Algarve Cup in Portugal, a big tournament with the best teams in the world there, and, for one game, we had more people on our bench than were watching. Maybe there were twenty people there."

Soccer has been a hard sell in the United States. Although it is No. 2 participation sport among youths, it has not taken a foothold among spectators, except, perhaps, when Pelé came to play for the Cosmos in the 1970's or during the 1994 Men's World Cup, whose legacy became the struggling MLS.

Still, there were indications that both this team and this event were something special. Mia Hamm, the world's best player, was already a star—she had even appeared in Gatorade commercials with Michael Jordan. David Letterman had adopted the U.S. squad, featuring "Soccer Mamas" regularly on his television show. Except for a strategically placed soccer ball, Chastain had posed in the nude for a GEAR magazine pictorial. ABC and ESPN committed significant air time to the World Cup.

And ticket sales were brisk.

Yet there always seemed to be that caveat: *Women's* soccer.

"If that type of thinking exists," said Marla Messing, President of the World Cup organizing committee, "we'll just have to charge right through it."

The charge began just before the tournament did, when organizers announced that the opening game was a sellout.

"The sellout is a great testimony to women's soccer," Chastain said. "I don't think anybody thought

> "The sellout is a great testimony to women's soccer," Chastain said. "I don't think anybody thought from the beginning that this could be a breakthrough event.

But NBC, which televised the Atlanta Olympics, ignored the game.

And, yes, this group was far superior to the team the United States sent to the 1998 men's World Cup in France, where the Americans finished dead last among thirty-two nations.

from the beginning that this could be a breakthrough event. I think we were really sticking our necks out on the line and putting ourselves out to be chopped down."

Added teammate Shannon MacMillan, "When they asked us if we thought the World Cup should be in big stadiums or smaller ones, we said, 'we'll pack the large ones."

How did the women approach this monumental event, which would be staged before 78,972, at the time the biggest gathering for women's sports?

"We were acting like a bunch of twelve-year-olds," Chastain said. "It was like a camp mentality. We were painting our nails, singing, and we even had a dance party [at the hotel]."

With thousands of kids—male and female—joined by their parents in a celebration of American sports, the U.S. squad beat Denmark 3-0. And on this Saturday in June, it was among the lead items on SportsCenter and

By now, America was catching on. Tickets were selling so well that organizers began expanding capacities, opening up areas of stadiums previously unavailable to the public . . . Suddenly, this was more than a world soccer tournament. It was a catalyst for women's sports. It was the focal point of an athletic revolution whose effects would last well into the next century.

in sports sections around the country.

"This is a huge tribute to them," Messing said. "I'm impressed and I couldn't be happier professionally. To me, it's all about the World Cup, and what we're really striving to achieve is to create that World Cup atmosphere. I think we succeeded."

Messing estimated that the double-header—Brazil played Mexico in the nightcap—had a gate of about $4 million.

"This is very positive for the Women's World Cup and for the sport in the future," she said. "There are a lot more families and a lot more children [than at the 1994 men's World Cup]. The crowd was mainly soccer families, the grass roots soccer community. There's a lot of hope for women's sports."

By now, America was catching on. Tickets were selling so well that organizers began expanding capacities, opening up areas of stadiums previously unavailable to the public. Media representation skyrocketed, with more than 2,000 accreditations issued. Other television networks—not just the sports outlets—began to take notice.

Suddenly, this was more than a world soccer tournament. It was a catalyst for women's sports. It was the focal point of an athletic revolution whose effects would last well into the next century.

The Americans beat Nigeria 7-1 in their next game, and with each goal came a profound understanding that this team's impact would rival that of the 1980 Olympic hockey team. Those college kids revitalized America's spirit with their stunning miracle on ice, but these twenty women were going to transcend their sport and make the 1999 Women's World Cup as significant a part of the sporting pantheon as any other in the 20th century.

That realization manifested itself not just at the stadiums, which were full for U.S. games and well-attended when other teams played, but at the practices.

On the day before their final first-round game against North Korea in Foxboro, Massachusetts, the U.S. women worked out at Babson College in nearby Wellesley. Unlike the sparse crowds that had attended previously, at least 300 fans showed up and were treated to a long autograph session following the workout.

"We'll stay and sign autographs and talk to the fans because we want to do it, not because someone tells us we should. It's important to them and it's important to us," said Tiffeny Milbrett.

Television crews from NBC, Fox, and CNN joined the regulars from ESPN. Newspaper and magazine columnists were showing up, tripling print media representation.

"We've always said we're America's best-kept secret," Foudy said with a chuckle. "Looks like the secret is out."

Indeed. As the Americans beat the Koreans 3-0 to secure their place in the second round, Foxboro's stadium was a sea of red, white, and blue.

From the time the U.S. women stepped onto the field for warm-ups until the last seconds of their victory, the crowd chanted "U-S-A! U-S-A!", performed the wave, and screamed encouraging words of support for their new role models.

"This tournament demonstrates that women can play at the international level," said Carrie Taylor, a former University of Michigan soccer player attending the game. "I'm hoping this will translate to a women's professional league."

That couldn't happen until after the 2000 Olympics in Sydney, but it certainly was on the minds of the players. And not just the Americans in the World Cup.

"If this tournament is successful," said Pretinha, Brazil's wonderfully creative forward, "it means we could come to play professional in the United States. Then it will be a World Cup that has benefitted women all over the world."

While a U.S.-based professional league wasn't foremost on their minds, the U.S. players admitted that it was important. Even if their success could carry the World Cup beyond expectations—as it was doing—could it translate to a professional league?

"The next step is to have a league of our own," Chastain said. "We really don't have a place to stay sharp. Without a place for our young players to play, it will be hard for us to be as successful."

U.S. women who have exhausted their college eligibility have had to play for clubs abroad when the national team is not on tour. That has been a difficult and financially unrewarding process.

"Right now, our younger players have to choose, 'Do I go into another career or do I starve and stay in soccer forever?'" said Lauren Gregg, an assistant coach with the national team.

The U.S. women weren't exactly starving in their pursuit of the World Cup. With the exception of defender Lorrie Fair, who kept her eligibility at North Carolina and would lead the Tar Heels to the 1999 national title, each would wind up making a $50,000

" We understand how significant our success and a successful World Cup could be," goalkeeper Briana Scurry said. "Knowing the women on this team, we're not going to back down from that kind of challenge. "

bonus in addition to her salary or stipends. But they understood that their success could lead to a veritable feast for their sport—at least in comparison to what was previously available.

"This tournament has demonstrated how our sport is growing all over the world," Messing said. "It's been like a cultural shift and, the way the tournament caught fire, we've tipped into something. We think this will be a seminal moment that people will look back in twenty years and say, 'That event is responsible for the development of women's sports.'"

Could they be the difference-makers, the pioneers? Women's sports already had made inroads, particularly at the 1996 Olympics. But this was different: the Olympics have a certain cachet that guarantee their acceptance and popularity. The Women's World Cup and women's soccer had none of that.

If this team and this event could not only make America take notice but take heart in the cause of furthering women's sports, well, sure, the Americans were ready to be pioneers.

"I can't say we haven't thought about it," goalkeeper Briana Scurry said. "We understand how significant our success and a successful World Cup could be. Knowing the women on this team, we're not going to back down from that kind of challenge."

The next on-field challenge was against a formidable German team that would be more physical than any the United States had faced. And when Chastain's errant backpass wound up in her own net, the Americans needed to rally.

They would do so—twice, for a 3-2 win.

Playing before 54,642 fans—including President Clinton, his wife Hillary, and daughter Chelsea—in Landover, Maryland, Chastain made up for her mistake and Fawcett also scored, both off corner kicks. The game, which helped cause a twenty-mile backup leading to Jack Kent Cooke Stadium, wasn't a sellout,

but nearly 14,000 tickets were sold in the three days between the victory over North Korea and the kickoff in the Washington suburb.

When Fawcett volleyed in her goal, Clinton leaped from his seat in celebration. And when he met with the American players in their locker room, they chanted "CLINTON! CLINTON!" as he posed for a group picture.

"He told us what an inspiration the team was, coming from behind," Foudy said. "I told him thanks for coming, it makes a ton of difference for this team. And we invited him back."

The team that was making "a ton of difference" for the women's sports movement headed to California for a replay of the most memorable game in U.S. soccer history.

On July 4, 1994, the host U.S. team played powerhouse Brazil before a sellout crowd at Stanford Stadium in the men's World Cup second round. Although the Brazilians won 1-0, the Americans acquitted themselves well against the nation that had won three world championships and, a few weeks later, would add a fourth title.

The magical feeling of that day could never be duplicated. Or could it?

Thanks to some enlightened scheduling—and, not to be overlooked, some fortunate on-field results—the Women's World Cup found itself with a United States-Brazil semifinal at Stanford on Independence Day.

"I'm aware of the significance of the date," said Sissi, Brazil's midfield star. "I only hope we can achieve the same results as the men did. We're going to shoot for it."

Had Sissi been a man, her soccer exploits would have made her a national icon in Brazil and a superstar throughout the world. Instead, she has had to survive in an environment where women's soccer is considered a third-rate endeavor, one in which even senior (as in "over-the-hill") men's leagues draw more attention.

As recently as the early 1990s, Brazil's women had to raise funds to travel to international tournaments because the soccer federation would not provide support.

"Only now do we get any notoriety,'" Sissi declared. "We were told ESPN Latin America was televising these games live, but we don't know if that is so."

Of course, a victory over the Americans and a trip to the final game would draw plenty of attention back home.

"It can only get better if we succeed," said Sissi.

The same could be said for the U.S. women.

The July 4th matchup was a bit confounding for the sport's greatest star, Pelé, who, not incidentally, has been involved in the promotion of women's soccer for

U.S. goalie Briana Scurry blocks a shot as teammate Joy Fawcett helps defend against Brazil's Prentinha in semifinals, July 4, 1999.

The game was a football festival, an Independence Day carnival, and a celebration of women's athletics before a crowd of 73,123. Many of the spectators were painted in red, white, and blue. They waved flags, carried banners, and chanted the names of their favorite players

years. In fact, Pelé has commented on "the purity" of the women's game, contrasting it with the often conservative and rugged style of modern men's soccer.

"I'm in a very difficult situation," Pelé said. "My heart is with Brazil, but, on the other hand, I'm very happy the U.S. team has done so well. I was active with my soccer camps years ago and teaching 'the beautiful game' to young girls across the country. This leaves me in a very emotional state. I only wish this was the final."

Pelé sensed that the Women's World Cup would have far-reaching repercussions.

"I'm very pleased to see how much attention the tournament has received worldwide," he said. "The level of play has been fantastic, very open, just the way I like it. This tournament no doubt will provide a tremendous lift to women's soccer around the world."

The game was a football festival, an Independence Day carnival, and a celebration of women's athletics before a crowd of 73,123. Many of the spectators were painted in red, white, and blue. They waved flags, carried banners, and chanted the names of their favorite players.

Brazil's colorful contingent of fans marched into the stadium to the beat of samba drums. And even after a 2-0 loss to the United States, the Brazilians kept dancing.

Scurry was the hero of the day with a handful of spectacular saves. Once the Americans had secured a spot in the final, Scurry saluted the crowd.

"The fans definitely made a difference for me," said Scurry. "It's great to see the outpouring of people supporting us."

Hey, girl! You ain't seen nothing yet!

The Women's World Cup final was set for the Rose Bowl six days later. China had blitzed Norway in the other semifinal and would be a formidable opponent.

While the players attempted to focus on the title game, the event itself had transcended soccer. Screaming fans greeted the players at airports. Security around the team was increased significantly. The team bus now had police escorts and streets were blocked off to allow easy access to training facilities and the stadium.

Fans gathered outside the team hotel, and players needed to use aliases when they registered. The media contingent following the team, which numbered perhaps a dozen when the tournament began, had reached the hundreds. And at games, that number reached into the thousands.

"The last two weeks have been an absolutely exhilarating experience," Messing said in summing up the phenomenon that was the 1999 Women's World Cup. "As big as I thought this tournament could be, it has been bigger.

"We have established the FIFA Women's World Cup as a world-class, world-caliber, stand-alone event like no other in sports."

FIFA, the world governing body for soccer, is not easy to impress. But when it saw more than 85,000 tickets sold for the Rose Bowl final, it had to be satisfied. And when FIFA executives saw how Americans rallied around the event, they had to be thrilled with the future possibilities for what, in many soccer officials' minds, had been a minor-league tournament.

"It's been a stupendous tournament," FIFA spokesman Keith Cooper said. "It's the level of enthusiasm, which is partly due to the success of the American team and the media reaction. If others are smart, they should think this stuff is hot and learn from USA '99 and see how the game has gained respectability and popularity."

Cooper would have been flabbergasted by the scene at Pomona-Pitzer College in Claremont, California, just hours after he spoke. As the U.S. team arrived for practice, it was greeted by a raucous crowd of more than 2,000.

"It's a blast for us," MacMillan said. "They were cheering and chanting our names the whole time. When the bus pulled up, they ran alongside; and when it moved up some more, they ran up some more. We had to have the policemen riding motorcycles by us just to get us to the field. It's great to see them share the enthusiasm," she added, pumping her fist.

"It's a real positive thing to see people looking to sports figures like these women as role models," said Lt. Gary Jenkins of the Claremont Police Department, a member of the motorcycle brigade handling security. "They've taken that role seriously and done a great job."

Behind him was a banner reading "GIRLS RULE!"

While the majority of the crowd was comprised of young girls, many of them wearing Mia Hamm jerseys, there was also a fair number of adults present. That impressed Scurry.

"You can't tell me the little girls are not dragging their parents here and dragging them to the games," she said. "The parents are seeing how soccer has taken off and they have done well in getting the kids out to the games. They feel their daughters should see quality soccer and they are seeing it in the World Cup."

Another sellout crowd would be on hand to see the culmination of this magnificent month. President Clinton would be there, too.

"We all kind of jumped out of our seats and were pumping our fists and yelling and cheering," Chastain

said after the team learned of the sellout and Clinton's plan to attend.

Clearly, this special group of women had achieved more than any of them could have imagined heading into the World Cup. They had become cover girls, lead news stories and celebrities. They had become the focal points of a movement that swept through the late 20th century, and they would be catalysts for the spiraling development of their sport—and all of women's sports—in the next century.

But they were not through.

Brandi Chastain *(center)* celebrates the game-winning overtime penalty shootout goal against China with teammates Sara Whalen *(left)* and Shannon MacMillan.

Brandi Chastain *(left)*, **Julie Foudy** *(center)*, **and team captain Carla Overbeck** *(right)* **celebrate after receiving their medals.**

GOOOOOOOOOOOOOOOOOOOAL!!!!!!!!!!
Chastain's left-footed blast soared into the net. She dropped to her knees as she ripped off her jersey and her teammates surged onto the field in delirious celebration. They hugged and rolled on the ground in a pile as pandemonium erupted in the stands.

And maybe women athletes everywhere in the world cheered, too.

There was much to cheer about, such as impressive television ratings: more than forty million Americans watched the final, a 0-0 tie capped by the 5-4 U.S. victory in the shootout.

There were appearances on every national television show imaginable, even Letterman *and* Leno. And a place on a Wheaties box cover.

Hundreds of endorsement opportunities came pouring in. And an autumn victory tour.

There was a White House visit and a collection of Sports Women of the Year awards.

And, last but not least, there was the lasting devotion of anyone who watched them or came into contact with them.

"It has been a privilege to coach this team," Tony DiCicco said. "Once I saw their passion for the game and the goals they set for themselves, it was fun to be around them. And it became a dream come true to end up their head coach.

> " The genuine pursuit of their dreams and goals is what is so enticing for people. It's kind of snowballed and turned into a wonderful phenomenon," Tony DiCicco said." They are finally getting their due. "

"Sportswomen of the Year" was the title given to the U.S. Women's Soccer team by *Sports Illustrated* magazine as shown on the cover of the December 20, 1999, issue.

"The genuine pursuit of their dreams and goals is what is so enticing for people. It's kind of snowballed and turned into a wonderful phenomenon. They are finally getting their due."

Or were they? The women boycotted a tournament in Australia the following January because they did not have new contracts from the federation. While a youth team went Down Under—and beat World Cup quality teams—the veterans stayed home, negotiating.

By late January, the women had secured a five-year contract even men's national teams would have found enticing: minimum monthly salaries of between $3,150 and $5,000, depending on experience, through the Sydney Olympics; $2,000 per game if the team plays three or more games in a month; bonuses of $1,000-$2,000 per win and $500 to $1,000 per tie in exhibition matches; a $700,000 team bonus for an Olympic gold medal; and team payoffs for making

the semifinals or winning the bronze or silver medal at an Olympics.

The deal also included paid maternity leave and child care.

Finally, as the rest of the world had so eagerly done, U.S. soccer officials recognized the team's achievement.

Hamm thought it was more than the players getting recognized. She knew who could really benefit most from the World Cup: the young women who were inspired by it all, the future Mia Hamms, Brandi Chastains and Briana Scurrys.

"We were those girls at one time and they can be there, too," Hamm said. "Whatever they want to be, whatever they dream to be, they can do it."

Women's World Cup Champions and "Soccer Mamas" Mia Hamm *(left)* and Brandi Chastain *(center)* appear as guests on *The Late Show* with David Letterman. *(right)*

"We were those girls at one time and they can be there, too," Hamm said. She knew who could really benefit most from the World Cup: the young women who were inspired by it all, the future Mia Hamms, Brandi Chastains and Briana Scurrys. "Whatever they want to be, whatever they dream to be, they can do it."

Mia Hamm ★ Forward

Mia Hamm has been called the greatest female soccer player in the world. She has made headlines with her bravura performances. As a young girl, however, Hamm was not the kind of person to attract attention to herself.

"In class, I wasn't the one who raised her hand all the time," she recalled. "I wasn't the most popular. I wasn't Miss Congeniality."

Hamm was admittedly moody, with a fiery temper. Her mother, a dancer, thought Mia could channel her energies as a ballerina. Hamm found a different way.

"Sports was a really good way for me to meet people, an easy way to express myself," she said.

To Hamm, her young life seemed like a continual road trip. Her father was an Air Force colonel who kept moving around the world with his wife and six children. Mia always had a soccer ball in tow. In some ways, a soccer field was the only place she felt at home.

From an early age her role model was her adopted brother, Garrett. Mia just wasn't his younger sister, she was his sidekick. Whenever he played soccer, he insisted that Mia play too. Pretty soon, she was outplaying many of the boys.

At age fourteen, Mia was discovered by Anson Dorrance, women's soccer coach at North Carolina and also coach of the U.S. women's national team. At fifteen, Hamm became the youngest player on the national team.

"Mia looked like a deer," remembered U.S. mid-fielder Julie Foudy, also a teenage member of that 1987 team. "She had those big brown eyes and a really short haircut, so her eyes were just huge. She reminded me of a deer caught in the headlights."

With Hamm's quick, darting moves, a deer on the field would have been a better analogy. Hamm later reunited with Dorrance at North Carolina, leading the Tar Heels in a dynasty that included four NCAA championships.

Hamm became an international celebrity after helping the U.S. team win the gold medal at the 1996 Olympics. A reluctant star, she has often tried to shift the spotlight to her teammates. After scoring her record 108th international goal in a game against Brazil in 1999, Hamm's reaction was typical.

"It was actually very reflective of our team, with lots of one-touch plays," she said, "and I was very fortunate to be on the end of it."

" In class, I wasn't the one who raised her hand all the time," she recalled. "I wasn't the most popular.

I wasn't Miss Congeniality. . . .Sports was a really good way for me to meet people, an easy way to express myself. "

First there was The Kick, then The Celebration. And no one had more reason to celebrate than Brandi Chastain.

Before delivering the winning goal at the '99 World Cup for the U.S. women's soccer team, she had had four years to think about why she missed out on the '95 tournament.

In 1991, Chastain had helped the Americans win the inaugural World Cup. But, four years later, she wasn't invited to join the team that would defend the title. Coach Tony DiCicco left her off because he questioned her work ethic and fitness.

"He said he was happy with the group he had, but said he'd keep me in mind," said Chastain.

Chastain was devastated but not discouraged. She quickly went to work and got in shape. She played in a professional league in Japan before joining a club team in Sacramento, California. Then she asked DiCicco for a second chance. He gave it to her, especially after the U.S. team failed to win gold in '95.

"I came into camp in great shape," Chastain said. "I think it made a difference."

DiCicco asked Chastain if she would be willing to switch from forward to defense. Chastain didn't hesitate— she would be willing to do anything to get back on the World Cup team.

"Brandi is a great story because she wouldn't give up her dream," said DiCicco. "There were no guarantees. But she went to Japan, and then all of a sudden she had the opportunity to go to an Olympic residency camp. She seized the moment."

And she seized the gold medal with the U.S. team at the '96 Olympics before making headlines at the World Cup three years later. None of her teammates was surprised that Chastain ripped off her shirt and exposed her sports bra after making the winning penalty kick against China. Chastain, a Californian with blond hair and a ready smile, goes by the nickname of "Hollywood."

"She can be dramatic at times," Scurry said with a wink.

Soccer has been a vital part of Chastain's life. At the University of California, she was named Soccer America's Freshman of the Year. But knee surgeries put her on the shelf for two years. She dropped out and eventually found her way to the women's powerhouse at Santa Clara, where she played for Jerry Smith—her future husband.

They were married in 1995, the same year that Brandi was struggling with rejection from the U.S. soccer team.

"I know what it was like for her not be involved all those years . . . how crushing, how devastating it was for her," Smith said.

Four years later, the devastation had turned to elation. But without Title IX, it never would have happened.

> "She can be dramatic at times," Scurry said with a wink. None of her teammates was surprised that Chastain ripped off her shirt and exposed her sports bra after making the winning penalty kick against China. Chastain, a Californian with blond hair and a ready smile, goes by the nickname of 'Hollywood.'

> "*h*ow many times do you have to prove that there's something to this?" said Donna Lopiano. "There's a big event, women prove themselves . . . guess what?—great athletes!"

The Women's Olympics

*t*here was Michael Johnson's searing speed and Andre Agassi's resurgence, culminating in a gold medal that rekindled his career.

But it was the women who seized the spotlight at the 1996 Atlanta Olympics and never once stepped out of it. Nothing could prevent women athletes from stamping the Games as their very own. On the basketball court, the soccer field, the softball diamond, and inside the gymnastic auditorium and the swimming pool competition among women surpassed expectations.

"These Olympics, probably more than any before, are showing a lot of little girls it's okay to sweat, play hard, and be an athlete," said tennis gold medalist Lindsay Davenport. "I've been watching the swimmers, the water polo, the basketball. The level of competition is incredible. It shows how far women's athletics has come just in my lifetime."

"These Olympics, probably more than any before, are showing a lot of little girls it's okay to sweat, play hard, and be an athlete," said tennis gold medalist Lindsay Davenport. "I've been watching the swimmers, the water polo, the basketball. The level of competition is incredible. It shows how far women's athletics has come just in my lifetime."

The women's softball team had their share of stars, too. From in-fielder Dot Richardson, an orthopedic surgeon, to powerhouse pitchers Lisa Fernandez (left), Michele Granger, and Michelle Smith, the Americans were attracting big crowds and headlines, and getting big results.

Sheryl Swoopes *(right)* **holds Ruthie Bolton as she cries tears of joy after winning the gold medal in the women's basketball at the 1996 Centennial Summer Olympic Games in Atlanta. The U.S. defeated Brazil 111-87.**

Sheila Cornell *(center)* **of the U.S. women's softball team is mobbed by teammates Dot Richardson** *(left)* **and Laura Berg** *(right)*
after Cornell hit a single to beat China 1-0 and advance to the championship game.

How far?

In 1972, the U.S. team at Munich had 342 men and ninety-six women. Every Olympics since, the number of women has soared while the percentage of representation for men has diminished. By Atlanta, there were 382 U.S. men and 280 women.

To put these figures within an even greater historical perspective, in the first half-century of the modern Olympics, from 1896 through 1948, there were 2,758 U.S. men and only 247 American women in the Games.

"I wasn't surprised that '96 would be a turning point in acceptance for women's sports," said Donna de Varona, a 1964 Olympic swimming champion who has dedicated her life to furthering the cause of women in sports. De Varona, who recently served as chairperson of the Women's World Cup, helped found the Women's Sports Foundation in addition to lobbying on behalf of Title IX compliance and more television coverage for women athletes. "It had been coming for a long time.

"There has always been a focus on elite athletes at

U.S. Women's Basketball team wear their gold medals during medal ceremonies at the 1996 Centennial Summer Olympic Games. Team members from left are: Jennifer Azzi, Lisa Leslie, Carla McGhee, Katy Steding and Sheryl Swoopes.

the Olympics. Through the years, especially in the age of television, you've had the spotlight on the Olga Korbuts, Nadia Comenecis, or Mary Lou Rettons in gymnastics. You had Jackie [Joyner-Kersee, in track]. There have been so many great individuals.

"For '96, we fielded the best teams ever, and they no longer were going against the systematic drug-induced athletes or totally supported-by-government athletes. This time, we were soaring because of the focus shifted to the females."

That focus shifted from day to day, although it never strayed far from the U.S. women's basketball squad, the real Dream Team in Atlanta. Sellout crowds not only flocked to their games, they showed far more interest in the women's game than they did the men's, which, because of its lopsided matchups between NBA All-Stars and amateur athletes, had become boring. The women's competition, on the other hand, was exhilarating to watch.

"I think they appreciate the way we always came out and fought hard," said guard Dawn Staley. Added

> "For '96, we fielded the best teams ever," said Donna de Varona, co-founder of the Women's Sports Foundation. "This time, we were soaring because of the focus shifted to the females."

teammate Lisa Leslie, "This was a special team and a special group of women."

The same could be said of the softball team. Although they had been the most dominant

U.S. Women's Basketball members Jennifer Azzi *(left)*, **Ruthie Bolton** *(center)*, **and Dawn Staley** *(right)* **celebrate with cartwheels after their 111-87 victory over Brazil at the Centennial Summer Olympic Games in Atlanta, August 4, 1996.**

team in the world for more than a decade, the American women sputtered, albeit temporarily, before roaring to the first Olympic gold medal in softball.

They, too, had their share of stars. From infielder Dot Richardson, an orthopedic surgeon, to powerhouse pitchers Lisa Fernandez, Michele Granger, and Michelle Smith, the Americans were attracting big crowds and big headlines, and getting big results.

Not even a preliminary-round loss to Australia could slow them. They avenged that stunning defeat with a win over China to end round-robin play. They later beat China for the gold.

Along the way, their enthusiasm, aggressive style, and supreme athletic skills captivated audiences. It made observers wonder why it took a decade to get softball onto the Olympic docket.

"We wanted to give people a chance to experience women's softball around the country and the world," said U.S. coach Ralph Raymond. "We wanted to show the youngsters just how this game should be played."

Did they ever!

"We've been referred to quite a bit throughout our careers as the Dream Team of softball," Richardson said. "We know the talent we have in this country. It's growing, it's exploding. You see the participation and the love of the sport and the dreams these young athletes have. Now these dreams include becoming a professional."

For the softball players and their basketball sisters, that dream became a possibility thanks to the success of the Atlanta Games.

A small-scale women's softball league surfaced in 1997, with hopes that a repeat performance by the Americans at the 2000 Sydney Olympics will lift the

Dot Richardson (center) of the U.S. Women's Softball team celebrates with teammates Laura Berg (right) and Lisa Fernandez after a two-run homer in the gold medal game against China.

profile of the sport even further and make a professional league more viable.

"It can't just be playing the game and winning it," Richardson said. "We need people watching the game and cheering for us to have an opportunity for the future."

While the softball players struggled to establish themselves as pros, the basketball players had no such difficulty. Sure, the creation of the ABL and WNBA made for one too many leagues—the ABL folded in its third season—but the WNBA quickly flourished. And it continues to grow in size, expanding its television contracts, and enjoying a solid Madison Avenue presence.

Of course, it helped immeasurably to have the prestige and marketing power of the NBA supporting the women's team and the women's basketball movement. It's something the NHL and Major League Baseball still need to recognize, and something it took FIFA another three years to fathom until the spectacular 1999 Women's World Cup.

OLYMPIC CHAMPION
Dot Richardson ★ Softball Shortstop

Both on and off the field, Dot Richardson has realized her goals in life.

"I always dreamed of being a surgeon," said Richardson, who now practices orthopedic medicine. "But I always had dreams, too, of being in the Olympics."

Richardson was in the tenth grade when she dissected a cat in biology class and "found it kind of interesting." By that time, however, she was already a softball star playing for amateur teams in the Orlando, Florida, area.

Actually, she was discovered as a ten-year-old while out having a catch with her brother Kenny. A man walked up and asked Richardson if she'd like to join his Little League baseball team. Not waiting for Dot to answer, the man said: "Good! We'll cut your hair short and call you Bob."

Richardson, a shortstop regarded by many as the best woman playing fast-pitch softball, was only seventeen when she won her first gold medal at the 1979 Pan-American Games in Puerto Rico. A couple of Pan Am gold medals later—and years of backroom wrangling to get softball into the Olympics—she was competing in the 1996 Atlanta Games. It was a memorable year for Richardson, who also learned that she had been accepted at the University of Southern California's medical school.

Softball had always been a big part of Richardson's life. At UCLA, Richardson was a four-time All-American and named the NCAA Player of the Decade for the 1980s. For six years she played for the high-profile Raybestos Brakettes, first commuting to Connecticut from Louisville, Kentucky, and then from Los Angeles because of her medical commitments.

Few athletes were more dedicated. While preparing for the Olympics, she set up a small batting cage in her apartment and practiced at all hours of the day. Her discipline did not go unnoticed. It wasn't long before Richardson found a note one of her neighbors had taped to her door: "Please train for the Olympics a little earlier in the evening, thanks."

Finally being a part of the Olympics was an important moment in Richardson's life. She found the experience "awesome . . . bigger than life."

Which is what they had been saying about her performance on a softball field for many years.

OLYMPIC CHAMPION
Amy Van Dyken ★ Swimmer

formed herself into an elite prep school swimmer who later became a junior Olympic champion, narrowly missing the 1992 Olympic team.

By 1995, Van Dyken was setting world records in the 50 freestyle. About the same time she was also answering questions about her possible use of banned substances. In the wake of doping scandals involving the dominant East German and Chinese swim teams of the 1980s and 1990s, officials were on the alert for the use of performance-enhancing drugs.

After a winter meet in France, the question came up. The answer? Van Dyken's approved asthma medication.

"I'm not out there slapping veins and shooting up," said Van Dyken. "I'm just trying to survive."

At the '96 Games, she did more than that, winning individual gold medals in the 50-meter freestyle and the 100-meter butterfly, and team golds in the 400 freestyle relay and 400 medley relay. It was the first time an American woman had won four gold medals at one Olympic competition.

Characteristically humble about her accomplishment, Van Dyken said: "If I can do it, anybody can."

She would have a hard time convincing anyone of that.

For Amy Van Dyken, just making the U.S. national swimming team would have been affirmation enough of the power of the human spirit. She didn't have to win an unprecedented four gold medals at the 1996 Olympics to prove the point.

Van Dyken overcame seemingly insurmountable odds just to get to Atlanta in the first place. As a child, she suffered from an asthmatic condition that seemed unlikely to permit athletics. Amy was six when a doctor suggested that she might try swimming as a form of exercise and social interaction. No matter that she was allergic to chlorine, or that she was unable to swim long distances because of her asthma. She was unable to swim the length of a pool until she was twelve. "It didn't matter that I wasn't good, because I was with my friends, doing what they were doing," Van Dyken said.

Amy was thirteen when she won her first race, a 50 freestyle. She wasn't swimming long races, but she looked excellent in short bursts. As she grew, she added muscle and then some confidence. The self-described "dork" trans-

Women were making huge strides as athletes, with Atlanta the coming-out party for many teams and individuals.

In the year of the female Olympian, swimmer Amy Van Dyken was chosen as the U.S. Olympic Committee's Sportswoman of the Year. With her four gold medals in the 50-meter freestyle, the 100-meter butterfly, and two relays, Van Dyken beat out the likes of Davenport, Richardson, Mia Hamm, and Shannon Miller. Until Van Dyken came along, no U.S. woman had won more than three gold medals in a single Olympics.

The women's gymnastics squad won gold in dramatic fashion. Although her vault was not the decisive performance in the competition, Kerry Strug's courage in making it with a badly injured left ankle left viewers gasping. And when she was carried to the medals ceremony by coach Bela Karolyi, viewers were left with fond memories of the teenage girl with the heart and soul of a champion.

Track and field, always a favorite with fans during the Olympics, in many ways became the province of the women in the 1990s. At Atlanta, it was the swan song for the great Jackie Joyner-Kersee, a coronation for Gail Devers, and an affirmation of the greatness of

. . . Kerry Strug's courage in making it with a badly injured ankle left viewers gasping. And when she was carried to the medals ceremony by coach Bela Karolyi, viewers were left with fond memories of the teenage girl with the heart and soul of a champion.

Jackie Joyner-Kersee *(left)* is consoled by her husband and coach, Bobby Kersee, after she withdrew from the heptathlon competition at the 1996 Centennial Summer Olympics in Atlanta. Bravely, Jackie insisted on competing in the long jump. Her decision appeared to be a mistake when, heading into her final jump, Joyner-Kersee found herself in sixth place.

Russia's Svetlana Masterkova. Except for the record-setting performances of Johnson, the women provided the greatest memories in '96.

Masterkova won the 800 meters and the 1,500, the first such double in twenty years. She did so with an impressive display of speed, power, and grace. For Joyner-Kersee, age and injuries had slowed her noticeably. She tearfully withdrew from the event she'd dominated, the heptathlon, with a sore hamstring. Bravely, Jackie insisted on competing in the long jump. Her decision appeared to be a mistake when, heading into her final jump, Joyner-Kersee found herself in sixth place.

Her heavily wrapped thigh throbbing in pain, she listened to the fans chanting her name and cheering her on.

"I thought I had this one chance," she said. "In the heptathlon there are seven events and you've got to do them all. This is just one. The crowd was unbelievable. I wanted to give them something to remember me by. I thought if the leg could hold on for one more jump . . . ."

Her last jump was 22 feet, 11 inches long. Good enough for the bronze medal. "I don't know where seven meters came from, but I'm glad it did," said Joyner-Kersee.

> The crowd was unbelievable.
>
> I wanted to give them something
>
> to remember me by, " said
>
> Joyner-Kersee. "I don't know
>
> where seven meters came from,
>
> but I'm glad it did.

Joyner-Kersee in the final of the women's long jump. Her last jump was 22 feet, 11 inches long, good enough for the bronze medal.

One of the most versatile of runners, Gail Devers was, like Joyner-Kersee, a UCLA graduate. She was a force in the dashes and the hurdles, and she would have won a 100-meter hurdles gold at Barcelona had she not stumbled a few steps from the finish. Though she won the 100 dash in Spain, Devers never received proper recognition for her achievement. She was known instead as the woman with the long, colorfully painted fingernails. Devers had been overshadowed throughout her impressive career by the great Marlene Ottey of Jamaica, who won seven Olympic medals, and by the Cuban Anna Quirot, who overcame severe burns to medal. A victory in the Atlanta dash would make Devers the world's fastest woman, the first to retain that title in twenty-eight years. Devers was already an inspiration, for she, too, had conquered pain and illness.

Devers missed the 1989 and 1990 track seasons with Graves' Disease, a life-threatening thyroid condition that sent her weight out of control. Her hair began to fall out and she was forced to use a wheelchair. At one point, her feet became so infected from an adverse reaction to radiation therapy that she could do little more than crawl. Doctors considered amputating her foot and told her she probably would never walk again. She could forget about running.

Then the medication and treatments took effect. Devers changed her diet and slowly began getting back into shape.

It wasn't long before she charged into the winner's circle. The Atlanta 100 would be her crowning achievement.

The race was over in a flash. Deciding a winner took a lot longer, however, with three women, including Ottey, bunched at the finish. Devers was one of them.

"I just waited and hoped," Devers said. "Standing there, waiting for them to name the winner, it felt like 1992 all over again."

In Barcelona the gold medal was decided between five runners. In Atlanta it was down to three: Devers, Ottey, or fellow American Gwen Torrence.

"I had no idea where I was or where anyone else was," said Devers. "I just wanted them to call someone's name."

The name they called? Gail Devers.

Were the 1996 Olympics a blessing for women's sports? Donna Lopiano, the director of the Women's Sports Foundation, is uncertain. But she remains hopeful.

"You know how soon we forget," she said. "All the hubbub around the '96 Olympics was women, women, women. Basketball, softball, soccer . . . it was so big.

"But there's no consistency to any of this. What women's sports needs more than anything in the next ten years is to break this log-jam of men's sports products on television and to get some good time-slot exposure on a regular basis for women's sports. That is absolutely crucial, because the economics of women's professional sports depends upon it.

"How many times do you have to prove that there's something to this? There's a big event, women prove themselves. You have twenty years of Title IX, twenty years of coaching, and—guess what?—great athletes! We're going to be there. And every chance we get, we're going to prove that women are great athletes."

The race was over in a flash. Deciding a winner took a lot longer, however, with three women, including Ottey, bunched at the finish. Devers was one of them. The name they called? Gail Devers. . . . After nearly two years of injuries, Olympic gold medalist Gail Devers (right) **runs to victory in her quarterfinal heat in the 100-meter sprint during the 1996 Olympic track trials.**

chapter three

"*W*hen I see anything that is challenging to me," says Marion Jones, "you can't stop me from going after it."

Great Women on the Track

*t*hey sped through barriers on and off the track. That they did so with such style, grace, power and determination made Wilma Rudolph, Wyomia Tyus, Florence Griffith Joyner and Jackie Joyner-Kersee the most inspirational of trailblazers.

Each won Olympic gold and the admiration of her fellow Americans as she made a name for herself in the world and played a part in making it better.

What Rudolph achieved on the track was an enduring testament to her ability as an athlete. What she accomplished off of it is worthy of a monument to the woman who overcame childhood illness and discrimination.

One of nineteen children, Rudolph grew up in a poor household in Tennessee. She contracted polio when she was four and lost the use of her left leg. Although the feeling in her leg returned thanks to massage treatments given by her siblings, she had to wear leg braces.

Rudolph was nine when she cast off the braces and began to walk without them. She wore a support shoe for two more years and was expected to be semi-disabled for her entire life.

Far from it. As a twelve-year-old, with all of that energy pent up inside her for so long, Wilma Rudolph was the fastest runner in town—even faster than the boys.

She rarely competed in the top track meets because, in the 1950s, racial segregation was still an issue; but Rudolph was so fast that she went undefeated in high school. Midway through, as a sixteen-year-old, she qualified for the Melbourne Olympics, winning a bronze in the 400-meter relay.

Four years later, no one could keep up with her as Rudolph romped in the 100-meter and 200-meter dashes. She also took the baton while trailing and sped the U.S. team to victory in the 400 relay.

"As I approached Wilma, I knew she wasn't taking off, so I yelled at her to go," said teammate Lucinda Williams-Adams. "And, finally, she took off and I gave her the baton, and it was like all the whirlwind had broke loose.

"We knew that if we got that baton to her, she would assist us in sharing that glory, because she was the hottest thing going."

Then, with her primary competitive years just ahead, she stopped running.

She turned to coaching and teaching after finishing college, serving also as a goodwill ambassador throughout the world.

She represented her country at the celebration of the tearing down of the Berlin Wall and established a foundation to promote athletics for the underprivileged.

In 1994, the woman who was often compared to Jesse Owens died of brain cancer.

> **We knew that if we got that baton to her, she would assist us in sharing that glory," said teammate Lucinda Williams-Adams, "because she was the hottest thing going.**

Wilma Rudolph wins the 4x100 meter relay for the U.S. at the 1960 Rome Olympics.

Wyomia Tyus was the next Tennessee State Tigerbelle to make Olympic history. Her three gold medals and one silver made Tyus a winner on the track. Her role as a goodwill ambassador and educator in emerging African nations made her a winner in life.

Dubbed "The World's Fastest Woman" after winning the 1964 and 1968 100-meter dashes—the first woman to successfully defend the title—she displayed her support for the cause of black athletes in Mexico City by wearing only black clothes. Her statement may not have been as controversial as the defiant salutes of Tommy Smith and John Carlos on the victory podium, but it was a genuine demonstration of her feelings and concern. As a further display of solidarity, she gave the medals she won to Smith and Carlos once they had been sent home early by the U.S. Olympic Committee.

Ed Temple, who coached the Tigerbelles and three U.S. women's teams at the Olympics, wasn't sure if Rudolph or Tyus was the superior runner.

"The most famous one was Wilma . . . maybe the outstanding one . . . I don't know," Temple said. "But maybe the best was Tyus. She was the first man or woman to repeat in the Olympic 100 or 200 meters— and the only one, until Carl Lewis got it by default" (when Ben Johnson was disqualified for steroid use after finishing first in the men's 100 at the 1988 Games).

Tyus quickly and easily moved into a second career as a teacher, counselor, and inspiration to young blacks and women. She also helped to organize the Women's Sports Federation.

Wyomia Tyus wins the women's 100-meter Olympic finals.

TENNESSEE STATE *Tigerbelles* ★ Track Team

The foundation for the great U.S. women's track and field teams of the last forty years was built by Ed Temple in Tennessee, far away from the bright lights and television cameras.

For more than a quarter century, the Tennessee State Tigerbelles, coached by Temple, ran away from the competition in college track and field. Many of the stars of America's Olympic teams, from Mae Faggs in 1952 to Chandra Cheeseborough in 1984, came from TSU. In between, there were such greats as Wilma Rudolph, who won three gold medals at the 1960 Olympics; Wyomia Tyus, winner of three golds and four Olympic medals overall; Martha Watson, a member of four Olympic squads; Madeline Manning, who came out of retirement three times to win championships; and Willye White, who competed in five—yes, *five*—Olympics.

These dedicated women faced many hardships over the years in order to compete in their sport. The Tigerbelles would drive twenty-two hours in a station wagon—with stops only for gas and fast food because the budget didn't include money for hotels—to get to the major meets at Madison Square Garden in New York. At many meets, they had to eat in segregated restaurants or dress in separate locker rooms.

On October 15, 1968, in Mexico City, she bettered the official world and Olympic records with a time of 11.0 seconds.

But they succeeded, forming the core of the U.S. women's sprint squads for decades.

Often they encountered obstacles in the least likely of places. During the first USSR-USA dual meet, the men's team, fearing embarrassment, demanded that their scores be kept separate from the women's. Then, at the 1964 Tokyo Olympics, the U.S. men's team wouldn't give Temple, coach of the women's team, clothes for a shot putter who couldn't fit into a woman's uniform. Furthermore, Temple's sprinters had to practice using Japanese starting blocks because the U.S. men, who had three, wouldn't lend them any.

"Those were the kind of things we had to battle," recalls Temple. "Unnecessary types of things. We, the women, were USA citizens representing the United States. Why did we have to go through all that kind of stuff? It just didn't make sense."

But they persevered and, at those Tokyo Games, the women won gold and silver in the 100 meters, gold in the 200, and a silver in the 400 relay.

Ever since, American women sprinters have been dominant. Much of the credit goes to the Tigerbelles for setting the precedent.

It would be almost two decades before such a dominant and inspirational American woman would reappear on the track: Florence Griffith Joyner. . . . Griffith Joyner took her status as a role model seriously, joining the President's Council on Physical Fitness and Sports in 1993. . . . It was a title that her sister-in-law, Jackie Joyner-Kersee also cherished . . . At fourteen, she knew she wanted to participate in the Olympics.

"Flo Jo" *(left)* wins the gold medal in the women's 100-meter final at the 1988 Summer Olympics in Seoul, Korea. Joyner-Kersee *(right)* competes in the women's long jump in the 1992 Summer Olympics in Barcelona, Spain.

It would be almost two decades before such a dominant and inspirational American woman would reappear on the track: Florence Griffith Joyner.

Ah, Flo Jo! With her painted fingernails and outlandish track suits—many of which she designed—Griffith Joyner was a fashion statement as she flew down the track.

And did she fly! At the 1988 Seoul Olympics, Flo Jo won three golds and a silver, setting world records in the 100 and 200 dashes. She didn't run to those remarkable marks, she *styled*.

"She accomplished amazing things on the track as well as off the track," observed sister-in-law Jackie Joyner-Kersee. "She had a sense of class about her. You couldn't take your eyes off her when she was running. She was special."

And she knew it. Flo Jo enjoyed her popularity as much as she enjoyed her sport.

"Looking good is almost as important as running fast," she would say. "If I look good, I feel good about myself and I perform well."

Griffith Joyner took her status as a role model seriously, joining the President's Council on Physical Fitness and Sports in 1993.

Five years later, after becoming a successful clothing designer, model, entrepreneur and author, Flo Jo died of a heart attack at age thirty-eight.

"What exactly is a role model? Is it someone trying to set positive examples for kids?" she once asked. "Then that's what I'm trying to do. I'm very happy to have that title."

> She accomplished amazing things on the track as well as off the track," observed sister-in-law Jackie Joyner-Kersee. "She had a sense of class about her. You couldn't take your eyes off her when she was running. She was special.

Coach Bob Kersee hoists Flo Jo in a victory celebration after she won the 100-meter dash at the U.S. Olympic Track and Field Trials in 1988.

Jackie Joyner-Kersee grimaces as she leaps the last hurdle during the women's heptathlon 100-meter hurdles during a rain storm at the 1996 Summer Olympics in Atlanta. *(left)*

It was a title that Joyner-Kersee also cherished, one that she sought even as a teenager: At fourteen, she knew she wanted to participate in the Olympics.

"I remember sitting home by the television, watching the 1976 Olympics, and we talked about how great it would be to be a part of it," she said.

Never did the kid from East St. Louis, Illinois, dream that she would one day own the competition. She made the Olympics her personal showcase in 1988 in Seoul when she broke the heptathlon points record with 7,291. (Her own record, by the way.)

No woman had scored 7,000 points before Joyner-Kersee, who was quickly heralded as the greatest female athlete in the world.

The heptathlon is a rugged two-day test of survival in seven events: the 100-meter hurdles, the high jump, long jump, and shot put; the 200-meter dash, the 800-meter run, and the javelin.

The gold medal proved an elusive prize for her, however. In the 1980 Olympic trials, she finished a distant eighth in the long jump. In the 1984 Olympics, she took home the silver when she was expected to win the gold.

"I let a hamstring injury defeat me," she explained. "But that was a blessing. It taught me to persevere."

Joyner-Kersee makes her second shot put in the women's heptathlon during the 1992 Olympics in Barcelona. *(left)*

Did it ever! At the 1988 Olympics, Joyner-Kersee over-came intense pain from a knee injury suffered during the high jump to win gold in a world-record performance.

On more than one occasion, Jackie was rushed from a meet to the hospital because of an asthma attack. At the 1995 USA Track and Field Championships, she won the heptathlon while wearing a mask to shield her against pollen.

"Jackie [is] on another planet," said heptathlete Cindy Greiner. "I competed with her in Houston when it was 123° on the track and our fingers were blistering in the shot put. She set a world record there. She refuses to let things bother her."

Jackie Joyner grew up in very modest surroundings in a family that, in her words, "barely made ends meet." From an early age she endured her share of hardship. "We had a roof over our heads, but at times there were no meals on the table or there was no heat. I didn't like the idea of wearing my clothes back to back, or not having fancy shoes, or not being able to go to the movies. But I understood that my father and mother were doing the very best for us."

Jackie was one of four children born to Mary and Alfred Joyner. She was not the only track star in the family, however. Her brother Al would also make a name for himself in the sport and marry Florence Griffith.

Jackie was an athlete for all seasons, playing basketball and volleyball as well as starring in track at Lincoln High. She went to UCLA on a basketball scholarship, starting all four years for the Lady Bruins. It was on the track, however, that she reached the top. She won the NCAA heptathlon championship three times and the Broderick Cup as America's top female athlete.

Her grace and style captivated UCLA assistant track coach Bob Kersee, whom she eventually married. Bob not only became her husband but a personal trainer and career director.

In 1986, she became the first woman to exceed 7,000 points in the heptathlon, with a 7,148 total at the Goodwill Games in Moscow. Later, she topped that with 7,158 at the U.S. Olympic Festival in Houston before her splurge in Seoul.

Since then, the Kersees have established a foundation to help underprivileged children and worked to rebuild the inner city of East St. Louis.

"My hope is to give some youngsters the opportunities I had," she said. "That's as important to me as any medals I might have won."

With Jackie Joyner-Kersee recently retired as "the world's greatest female athlete," it hasn't taken long for another American to begin filling her shoes. Welcome, Marion Jones.

Not so fast, you say?

Yes, very fast. Jones is not only the fastest runner in the world today but she has all the makings of a pro basketball star. And don't think the WNBA isn't interested.

"She is the most complete athlete that I have ever worked with, and that includes being an assistant Olympic coach," says Sylvia Hatchell, who coached Jones on the University of North Carolina women's basketball team.

So far, not too many opponents have been able to beat Jones to the finish line. As a prep track phenom in California and a two-sport star at North Carolina, Jones had already made an impact on the women's sports scene. Then in 1997 she leaped to the top in track and field as the U.S. and world champion in the 100 meters. She was also the American long jump champion.

In winning the long jump title, Jones dethroned none other than the redoubtable Joyner-Kersee. And Jones' time in the 100 meters was second-best in women's track history behind another pretty good runner, Florence Griffith Joyner.

There's more. In 1998, Jones didn't lose a single sprint race. And she only lost one long jump competition—in her very last meet of the year, when she finished second to Germany's Heike Drechsler.

"She runs like a man," said British Olympic star Linford Christie, offering a compliment. "When she comes out of the blocks, she's very low. That's what generates your speed."

The 5-foot-10 Californian was fifteen when she made her first big splash on the prep track scene in 1991, breaking the national high school record in the 200 meters. One month later, she won the 100, 200, and 400 all in one glorious afternoon at the California divisional finals. "It was like a Jesse Owens day," said Brian FitzGerald, who coached Jones at Rio Mesa High School in Oxnard, California, during her freshman and

In winning the long jump title, Jones dethroned none other than the redoubtable Joyner-Kersee. And Jones' time in the 100 meters was second-best in women's track history behind another pretty good runner, Florence Griffith Joyner.... In 1998, Jones didn't lose a single sprint race. . . . "She runs like a man," said British Olympic star Linford Christie, offering a compliment.

sophomore years. "And a lot of people wanted a piece of her."

But Jones was unable to compete at the college level until a technical mix-up over drug testing was cleared up in the courts. Then it was on to North Carolina on a basketball scholarship.

"I loved track, and I wanted to keep it like that," Jones said. "So many young runners get burned out. I figured I'd do both, but in the beginning I needed discipline and the Carolina basketball program is very well structured."

A forward in high school, Jones made the Tar Heels as a point guard. Her speed was an obvious asset on the basketball court. "Every loose ball she got," said former Tar Heels strength coach Jeff Madden. "She'd be ten yards ahead of everybody when she got the ball and fifteen yards ahead when she shot it."

Sparked by Jones, the Tar Heels won the 1994 national championship. No sooner had the NCAA basketball playoffs ended than Jones was competing in the NCAA track championships, finishing second in the long jump. But it wasn't until after graduation that Jones became an internationally renowned track star. And it happened so quickly.

In the summer of 1998, Jones twice ran the 100 in 10.71, the fastest time of any woman in track history with the notable exception of Griffith Joyner. She also long-jumped a world-leading 23'11" at one meet and won the 100, 200, and long jump in another, becoming the first woman in fifty years to win three individual events in one meet. Jones would improve on her 100 with a 10.65 clocking—an extraordinary time, but still behind Griffith Joyner's record 10.49.

Unable to compete in the 1996 Olympics because of a broken foot, Jones had a game plan for her future: first the Olympics and then a couple of years in the WNBA.

"When I see anything that is challenging to me, you can't stop me from going after it," she says.

Marion Jones wins the women's 100-meter race with a time of 10.84 at the Gugl-Meeting in Linz, Austria, 1998.

SPRINTER ★ HURDLER ★ JUMPER
Fanny Blankers-Koen

A team unto herself, Fanny Blankers-Koen is the greatest female athlete Europe has produced.

Blankers-Koen had no challengers. The Dutchwoman would often be compared to Babe Didrikson Zaharias—they both competed at the 1936 Los Angeles Games, although Fanny managed just a sixth place finish in the long jump while Babe won two golds and a silver in other events.

Because the Games were suspended during World War II, Blankers-Koen had to wait twelve years for another shot at Olympic glory. By then, she was a mother with two children; but she was the one who held world records in the 100, the 80-meter hurdles, the long jump, and the high jump.

Blankers-Koen stuck to the sprints because an IOC rule, which Olympic organizers claimed protected women from too much physical stress, limited her participation in the Games. She ran the 100 and 200, plus the hurdles, and took part in the 400-meter relay. A heavy workload, for sure, but she wasn't one to back off.

"I took it as a personal challenge to win each of those races," she said. "There were men who had done such things, great men like Jesse Owens. I felt a woman could do the same."

She was right. Blankers-Koen won the 100-yard dash, the 200, and the hurdles before carrying the Netherlands to the relay gold.

She continued training for another four years, her eye on more gold at the 1952 Games. But, at thirty-four years of age and with the strain of training and competition having taken a toll on her body, she became injured and could not qualify for the Helsinki Olympics. Regardless, Fanny Blankers-Koen had earned her place not only as a great female athlete but, in a manner of speaking, as a great national track team.

> " I took it as a personal challenge to win each of those races," she said. "There were men who had done such things, great men like Jesse Owens. I felt a woman could do the same. "

Mrs. Fanny Blankers-Koen, who won three individual Olympic titles, is shown *(left)* breaking the tape in the 400-meter relay to win her fourth Olympic medal as a member of the Dutch relay team August 7, 1948 in London, England.

"*a* lot of us had to identify with male athletes growing up," said Tina Thompson, a forward for the Houston Comets. "Now these little girls have us."

Girls of Summer

*a*fter another rousing victory, the bus carrying the U.S. women's national basketball team pulled out from the Providence Civic Center when a young girl started to chase the bus, waving an autograph book. The bus picked up speed as the girl, her eyes welling with tears, tried valiantly to catch up.

Some of the players spotted her and had the driver stop the bus. One by one, the players stepped off to greet the young fan. They didn't resume their trip until all of them had signed her book.

The enthusiasm of this young fan would mirror the popularity of women's basketball, particularly after the U.S. team had won the Olympic gold medal in 1996 and inspired not one but two pro leagues.

Fast forward three years later to a Women's National Basketball Association (WNBA) game in

Pat Summitt ✫ Head Coach

Pat Summitt with Chamique Holdsclaw.

Pat Summitt is driven. Some would say she's in overdrive. Always has been. Always will be.

When she first took over as basketball coach of the Lady Vols in 1974, women's basketball was a low priority at the University of Tennessee, as it was at most universities in the country. In Summitt's first game as coach, only fifty people were in the stands. Summitt was determined to change things.

Once the Lady Vols started winning, the fans started coming. Six NCAA Championships, sixteen Final Four appearances and more than 700 victories later, the Lady Vols were averaging approximately 15,000 fans a game.

Talk about perfection! Her 1998 national champions went 39-0! Two years later, the Lady Vols came close to winning another championship but lost to the University of Connecticut Lady Huskies in the 2000 NCAA final. Having produced winning teams consistently, it's no surprise that Summitt's program has become the envy of schools everywhere.

"Pat is the best in our business," says Louisiana Tech women's basketball coach Leon Barmore. "Pat Summitt can coach any team of any sex at any level." High praise, considering Barmore had the leading winning percentage in the women's game.

Because Summitt is so uncompromising and driven, she has been called other, less complimentary things as well. "She is tough to play for sometimes,"Kellie Jolly said. "As a player, you know when you go to Tennessee that you're going to play for a perfectionist, someone who's going to be very demanding."

Summitt has always been a hard worker, one who has imparted her work ethic to her teams. She grew up on a farm in Henrietta, Tennessee, playing basketball in a hayloft with her brothers—but only after the farm work had been done. She was an athletic, high-flying player at the University of Tennessee-Martin. Later, she helped the U.S. Olympic team win a silver medal as a player and a gold medal as a coach.

Summitt's program is one that other schools use as a role model. Her Tennessee teams have been at the forefront of the surging women's college basketball movement, demonstrating that women don't have to take a back seat to men when it comes to drawing an audience and producing revenue. Ten of her players have gone on to play in the WNBA.

Basketball has been the only team sport with a strong tradition of women coaching women. Other trailblazing coaches in women's basketball include Sandra Berenson, Vivian Stringer, Bertha Teague, Tara VanDerveer, Margaret Wade, Billie Moore, and Jody Conradt.

New York's Madison Square Garden. The Washington Mystics were playing the New York Liberty.

During pre-game warm-ups, a young female fan sat riveted with fascination while guard Chamique Holdsclaw went through her paces. The fan wore Holdsclaw's college jersey from Tennessee.

"She was there just to watch Holdsclaw warm up," said Pat Summitt, Holdsclaw's college coach. "She wouldn't take her eyes off her. Ten years ago, women wouldn't have had a pro game in the Garden. And you certainly wouldn't have had a young kid watching every move that someone like Chamique makes."

Women basketball players were creating this kind of attention all over the world in the '90s. In this new age for women's sports, basketball was suddenly taking center stage. It began with a spate of strong collegiate programs around America and took flight with the success of the 1996 U.S. Olympic basketball team.

A collection of the best women's basketball talent in America, the fan-friendly Olympians played on four continents and covered more than 102,000 air miles on their pre-Olympic barnstorming tour. With so much experience competing as a team at the international level, the Americans came back to sweep the Olympic tournament in Atlanta and take the gold medal, compiling a remarkable 60-0 record along the way.

Forget Michael Jordan, here came Sheryl Swoopes. Swoopes, a college star at Texas Tech, was now an international celebrity with her own brand of Nike sneaker. Other shoe manufacturers were lining up as well to negotiate endorsements with the victorious Olympians.

No, it wasn't likely that Lisa Leslie, Rebecca Lobo, Jennifer Azzi, and Dawn Staley were about to leap past Jordan in celebrity status. But they would become unique in another way when their popularity sparked interest in establishing a professional women's basketball league.

Actually, two leagues.

The American Basketball League (ABL) and the Women's National Basketball Association (WNBA) were spawned by the Olympians' success and popularity. The ABL came first, then the NBA-backed WNBA started flexing its muscles about eight months later. The ABL, which played in the winter, existed on a smaller budget and, for the most part, was based in smaller towns. The WNBA, a summer league, not only had the full backing of the NBA but also the use of its facilities and, in many cases, its management.

"I was in Atlanta: I could sense something powerful was going on, and so could a lot of other people," said Leonard Armato, a sports agent whose clients included NBA stars Shaquille O'Neal and Hakeem Olajuwon. "Twenty years ago, women were cheerleaders. Now, it's okay to be an athlete."

Women basketball players were suddenly sharing the front pages of the sports section with the men. And they had options.

Jennifer Azzi took the path to the ABL, signing with the San Jose Lasers. "It just felt like the right thing to do and the right thing for women's basketball."

But the ABL had problems. It was underfinanced and overshadowed by the WNBA, which had the advantage of built-in name recognition.

Kate Starbird, who played for the Seattle Reign, said that anonymity "was one of the hardest things about being in the ABL. We were all proud of what we were doing, but just trying to explain to somebody else who just didn't get it was tough."

There were precedents for women's pro basketball leagues in America. The ill-fated Women's Professional Basketball League (WPBL) lasted only three years from 1978—1981 despite the presence of superb players such as Carol Blazejowski and Ann Meyers.

Greg Williams was one of the pioneers who believed in professional women's basketball. Yet, when he started as a coach, he had never watched a women's basketball game.

He was involved in the WPBL and, later, the Women's American Basketball Association (WABA), which lasted only one season. To him, establishing a new league was like landing on a faraway planet—you weren't quite sure you could survive.

"I used to say I don't know if I should be commended or committed," Williams said.

Williams was a star basketball player and an assistant coach at Rice in the 1960s. When he got the phone call to coach in the WPBL, he had left basketball and was in sales. His next stop: the Houston Angels and a championship ring. The Angels were the first of three teams to win championships in the league.

"Even though there were two other champions crowned in the WPBL, the league didn't have enough money to get them rings," he said.

Williams' team might have won a championship, but it still had money problems like other franchises in the league. On one occasion, the players had to

The original limousine

decide whether to play without the guarantee of being paid. One night before a game, Williams told his team: "We're leaving at 7 A.M. If five of you show up at the airport, we'll go. If we don't have five, we won't."

The Angels played their game.

Not long after, the league folded.

"To think the WPBL survived for three years is pretty amazing when in Houston, Texas, you didn't even have high school girls' basketball teams until 1978," Williams said. "Title IX was on paper, but it was being ignored."

Other leagues that followed had even less staying power. The Women's American Basketball Association lasted only one season. The Ladies Professional Basketball Association lasted only one month. And then there was the Liberty Basketball Association. With lower baskets, shorter courts and tighter spandex uniforms, the LBA couldn't stretch itself beyond one exhibition game.

Only the All-American Red Heads could boast of any permanence, and they did not play in a league. The Red Heads were, in essence, a female version of the Harlem Globetrotters. Wearing colorful uniforms to match their signature flaming red hair (which usually came out of a bottle), the Red Heads performed half-time shows that featured trick shooting, dribbling, and juggling, but, like the Globetrotters, they could also demonstrate a serious side to their basketball.

Originally created to promote a local beauty parlor chain in Missouri, the Red Heads became a national

of the "Red Heads," the long-running women's professional basketball team, shown at the Women's Basketball Hall of Fame.

America, the land of opportunity. Because she was a woman, Jennifer Gillom had to go to Europe to find it.

Like many other women basketball players, Gillom took the long way home before finding safe harbor in the WNBA. Gillom had been a basketball star at the University of Mississippi, and was good enough to play professionally. But a women's professional basketball league? Not in the United States—not when she was graduating.

"I felt my career would be over," Gillom remembered. "I was getting ready to apply for a job in coaching."

Then came a long-distance call: she could play in the Italian League. But Jennifer, a native of Abbeville, Mississippi, didn't want to leave home. Then again, it was her only chance to play professionally.

So, she went to Italy.

Playing for teams in Milan, Ancona and Messina, she learned a new version of the game. "The basketball in Italy is much more physical," Gillom said. "You want to jump in the Jacuzzi after every game. You saw bruises after every game. No blood, no foul—that's the way they play over there."

Before going to Europe, Gillom had considered herself a "finesse player."

"I hated contact. And, believe me, it changed my game all the way around. I relied on my little finger roll [which she had learned while watching her hero, Julius Erving], one-handed shots. I had to change my game to powering to the basket with both hands."

Gillom was a perennial selection to the Italian League all-star team and a two-time Most Valuable Player. Both before and during her time in the Italian League, she helped the U.S. national team win gold medals at the World Championships, Pan American Games, and Olympics.

She had accomplished everything she wanted—except to play professionally in front of her family in America. If only a viable professional league would open in the States before her career was over.

Then, just as she was about to give up, she received another long-distance phone call asking her to play for the Phoenix Mercury.

Welcome home, Jennifer. Welcome, WNBA!

sensation in 1936 when they began barnstorming across the country. Playing almost exclusively against men's teams, the Red Heads won approximately ninety per cent of their games. Orwell Moore, the Red Heads' longtime owner and coach, felt that good conditioning was the only way women could compete with men while playing under their rules.

Remarkably, the Red Heads lasted fifty years. They were inducted into the Women's Basketball Hall of Fame in 1999.

Los Angeles Sparks center Lisa Leslie *(left)* goes in for the lay-up in front of Sacramento Monarchs center Tajama Abraham during the second half of their WNBA game.

. . . it wasn't likely that Lisa Leslie, Rebecca Lobo, Jennifer Azzi and Dawn Staley were about to leap past Michael Jordan in celebrity status. But they would become unique in another way when their popularity sparked interest in establishing a professional women's basketball league. Actually, two leagues.

Except for a few semi-pro leagues here and there, women's basketball had been confined to college campuses and the Olympics throughout most of the 20th century. The sport had been relatively tame compared to the men's game until such players as Blazejowski, Meyers, and Nancy Lieberman came upon the scene. They had learned their games playing against men and brought a new intensity to women's basketball once rules changes took the shackles off them.

Women could now compete just like the men in a full court game—they could even dunk if they wanted to. Cheryl Miller became the first woman to do so, while playing at Southern Cal. Winning gold medals at the Olympics only increased the stature of American women around the world. They weren't the only female basketball players making waves internationally. When Uljana Semjonova led the Soviet Union to a gold medal in the 1976 games, she became an international star. Later she became the only non-American woman elected to the Basketball Hall of Fame.

The WPBL was a league before its time. The women's college game had not yet made itself part of the national consciousness, and many of its great players were hardly household names.

Though the ABL was generally conceded to have more talent, it didn't have what the WNBA had—the NBA's support. The ABL played in the traditional winter season, competing against the more established sports of football, college basketball, and hockey. The WNBA not only had better TV exposure and a higher profile, there were no major sports competing with it during the summer.

When the ABL folded in the middle of its third season, few were surprised. What happened next came as no surprise, either. Many of the ABL's top players headed for the WNBA, giving the league an even stronger talent base. The new WNBA arrivals had to adjust to a smaller ball and a concentrated thirty-two-game schedule played in less than eleven weeks. There were other adjustments that were easier to make, however.

"You go from staying at the Holiday Inn to the Ritz Carlton," said guard Kedra Holland-Corn, who went from San Jose in the ABL to Sacramento in the WNBA. "You go from having to go to a rental car place to rent two vans to having your big bus waiting for you at the airport. You go from taking your own bags to someone taking your bags for you."

Another pleasant surprise for Holland-Corn was the WNBA crowds. The league averaged 10,248 a game in the regular season in its first three years, exceeding most early estimates. One of the WNBA's proudest moments was the sold-out 1999 all-star game at New York's Madison Square Garden.

More than 4.5 million customers paid to see regular season WNBA games in the first three years as the league expanded from eight to twelve teams by 1999. Four more were added for the 2000 season, bringing the league total to sixteen teams, all in NBA cities.

Admittedly a work in progress, the WNBA has yet to convince everyone that it is here to stay. Doomsayers have pointed out that league attendance slipped from an average of 10,869 in the second year to 10,207 in the third. The league had 1,959,733 answers for that—the total number of fans that watched regular season WNBA games in 1999, a professional women's record.

In the three years of its existence, the WNBA had already matched the longevity of the WPBL and made an impact on the American sports landscape. Women no longer were second class citizens in professional sports. Be like Mike? What about Jennifer, Cheryl, or Rebecca?

"A lot of us had to identify with male athletes growing up," said Tina Thompson, a forward for the Houston Comets. "Now these little girls have us."

Though the ABL was generally conceded to have more talent, it didn't have what the WNBA had—the NBA's support. . . . When the ABL folded in the middle of its third season, few were surprised. What happened next came as no surprise, either. Many of the ABL's top players headed for the WNBA, giving the league an even stronger talent base.

> " **You go from staying at the Holiday Inn to the Ritz Carlton," said guard Kedra Holland-Corn, who went from San Jose in the ABL to Sacramento in the WNBA. "You go from having to go to a rental car place to rent two vans to having your big bus waiting for you at the airport. You go from taking your own bags to someone taking your bags for you.** "

Olympic gold medalists Rebecca Lobo *(left)* **and Sheryl Swoopes display their jerseys for the inaugural season of the WNBA .**

chapter five

> "She was my first idol," Retton said of Korbut. "She opened gymnastics to me. She showed emotion. She laughed when she won and she cried when she fell. I liked that."

Golden Gymnasts

*i*n terms of popularity, gymnastics is to the Summer Olympics what figure skating is to the Winter Games, a sport that enthralls all who view the competition. Olympic Gymnastics is a television gold mine, and three women can be thanked for it.

Olga Korbut was the first to bring worldwide attention to the sport, at the 1972 Games in Munich.

Viewers tuning in for the opening of the gymnastics competition could not have expected such enchantment, particularly from a seventeen-year-old Russian pixie who could bend her body like a pretzel, soar like an eagle, and light up any arena with her dimplish smile and playful demeanor.

A relative novice on the international scene, Korbut

Before Korbut captivated the world at Munich, 15,000 American girls were involved in gymnastics. Shortly after the 1976 Games, 150,000 were involved. . . . For all of Korbut's charms, she wasn't the gymnast Comaneci was. As if to punctuate her magnificence, Comaneci added perfect scores on the balance beam and uneven bars, winding up with seven in all.

was chosen as an alternate for the powerful 1972 Russian team. Yet she won three gold medals and a silver. Her mesmerizing moves on the balance beam—including a rare back flip—and her balletic yet robust tumbling in the floor event made her stand out from her more accomplished teammates.

The pigtailed Korbut really struck a chord with viewers when she cried after judges gave her a low score of 7.5 on the uneven parallel bars following a slip during the all-around competition. She enchanted fans even more when she rebounded the next day to win a silver medal on the bars in the individual event.

The first woman to complete a backward somersault on the uneven bars, Korbut's athletic skills, impish smile, and vivacious personality made for an irresistible combination. Suddenly, gymnastics had become a dynamic sport requiring speed, power, grace and charm.

And youth. By the 1976 Olympics, Olga had passed her prime as a gymnast, winning only a silver on the beam.

"I am twenty, not twelve," she said in Montreal. "Each new element is harder to learn. Sometimes it makes my flesh creep to go onto the platform."

But she had already made an impact. Before Korbut captivated the world at Munich, 15,000 American girls were involved in gymnastics. Shortly after the 1976 Games, 150,000 were involved.

Oddly, she was more popular in the West than back home, where Soviet sports officials frowned on elevating the individual to star status.

Romanian officials felt the same way about Nadia Comaneci.

Audiences who had witnessed Korbut's brilliant debut four years earlier at Munich fell quickly for the fourteen-year-old Comaneci. At the 1976 Games, the Romanian teenager earned three

"A ten was very nice," Nadia said with innocent understatement. "But I have received many of them before.

Nadia Comaneci performs her balance beam routine that led to a gold medal and a perfect score at the 1976 Montreal Olympics.

gold medals and the first perfect scores of ten awarded in Olympic gymnastic competition.

When Comaneci began her routine on the uneven bars, twisting and turning so rapidly and fluidly, the first perfect score in Olympics history seemed inevitable.

"A ten was very nice," she said with innocent understatement. "But I have received many of them before."

Nineteen to be exact, but never on such a huge stage, with the world watching and hoping for, well, another Korbut to come along.

For all of Korbut's charms, she wasn't the gymnast Comaneci was. As if to punctuate her magnificence, Comaneci added perfect scores on the balance beam and uneven bars, winding up with seven in all.

At Montreal she won three gold medals, a silver, and

made the most daring maneuvers seem commonplace in her routines.

Lauded as a heroine back home, Comaneci rarely ventured from behind the Iron Curtain, except to compete at the 1980 Olympics in Moscow, where she won a gold medal in the balance beam and floor exercise and a silver in the all-around and team events.

Most Americans ignored those Games because of the U.S. boycott. But they made sure to keep tabs on Comaneci.

What they saw was a maturing eighteen-year-old with the staying power to handle the younger kids. But Comaneci wasn't quite the gambler she'd been at Montreal.

Was the element of danger she introduced to the sport too great for her to compete with the younger athletes who now dominated the gymnastics competition? Did they comprehend how influential Comaneci had been in revolutionizing the sport?

Although Comaneci attended the 1984 Olympics as a coach, she rarely was heard from after the Moscow Games. By 1989, she was so disenchanted with life under the Ceausescu dictatorship that one night she walked six miles to the Hungarian border and defected to the West.

She later married Bart Conner, perhaps the greatest American male gymnast.

a bronze. Comaneci topped the podium in the all-around, balance beam and uneven bars, taking a bronze in the floor exercise. She and her Romanian compatriots finished second to the Soviets in the team competition.

She also carried the sport beyond its classical roots, turning it into a much more powerful, athletic event. Future gymnasts would need nerves of steel to compete at the international level once Comaneci

Mary Lou Retton on the balance beam during the 1984 Summer Olympics in Los Angeles.

The final step in the popularization of gymnastics came with the ascension of Mary Lou Retton in 1984. While many gymnastic powerhouses from Eastern Europe boycotted the Los Angeles Games, Retton came bouncing out of West Virginia with a wide smile, bubbly disposition, and a truckload of talent. The media immediately identified Retton as the rising star of those Games.

The 4-foot-9, sixteen-year-old Retton won the all-around title, spicing it with a perfect mark in her specialty, the vault. The first American woman to capture a gold medal in that event, she won four more medals: silvers in the team competition and the vault to go with the bronze medals she won in the floor exercise and uneven bars.

She was easily the most publicized woman at those Games. Retton became America's darling, appearing on dozens of talk shows and variety programs, the covers of magazines, and in commercials. She was selected the 1984 Female Athlete of the Year by The Associated Press, and in 1985 was the youngest inductee into the U.S. Olympic Hall of Fame.

Coached by Bela Karolyi, who guided Comaneci's career before he defected to the United States, Retton proved that an American athlete could elevate her sport in the same way her idols had done.

"She was my first idol," Retton said of Korbut. "She opened gymnastics to me. Russians were supposed to be stone-faced, but not Olga. She showed emotion. She laughed when she won and she cried when she fell. I liked that. That's like me. I show emotion."

As for Comaneci, Retton said she "loved the way she was so unafraid to try something. She challenged everyone else to do more, because Nadia was doing more."

"I hope our current gymnasts see me as someone who opened up the sport for Americans," Retton added. "First there was Olga and then Nadia and then, finally, there was an American, someone who proved that you didn't have to be an Iron Curtain athlete to win in this sport."

Nine years after becoming an American cultural icon and almost a decade after her last competitive event, a national poll asking who was America's No. 1 female athlete came up with the name Mary Lou Retton.

Talk about staying power.

> "I hope our current gymnasts see me as someone who opened up the sport for Americans," Retton added. "First there was Olga and then Nadia and then, finally, there was an American, someone who proved that you didn't have to be an Iron Curtain athlete to win in this sport.

"*i*f there was no Sonje Henie," says figure skating historian Dale Mitch, "there is no telling where skating might have headed."

Ice Queens

*f*or as long as anyone can remember, one sport has been the domain of women: figure skating. From Sonja Henie, Carol Heiss, and Peggy Fleming to Katarina Witt, Kristi Yamaguchi, and Michelle Kwan, the skating spotlight has nearly always fallen on the women.

Hard to believe, considering the way women got started in the sport.

Madge Syers dreamed of being a champion figure skater. Raised in an upper class English family, she began skating as a youngster and soon was the best women's skater in Britain.

She was also an uncrowned champion because, in the early 1900s, women were barred from competition. Officials who organized the world championships in 1896 felt it improper for a woman to compete in athletics. Though Syers' husband Edgar was an accomplished skater and the couple formed an outstanding pair, Madge wanted more.

In 1902, she filed an entry for the International Skating Union's World Championships, held in London. There was no scheduled women's competition and no female competitors other than Madge Syers. So organizers, citing no specific rule forbidding her from entering, allowed her to compete in the men's field, perhaps expecting her to flop embarrasingly.

"The courageous stand she took opened the way for every [woman] skater who followed," observed Heiss, the 1960 women's Olympic champion.

Syers didn't merely break the gender barrier at the beginning of the 20th century, she won a silver medal, beating every man (her husband included) except Ulrich Salchow, the defending champion and a legend in men's figure skating. The other men were, to say the least, astonished.

The British federation quickly approved women's skating, though it took four years to create a wo-men's division at the World Championships. Naturally, Syers won the competition in 1906 and again in 1907. She went on to win a gold medal at the 1908 Olympics and took a bronze with Edgar in pairs. She remains the only woman to win two figure skating medals at the same Olympics.

While Syers was the first pioneer in women's skating, Sonja Henie was a bonafide trail-blazer. She is the reason the Winter Olympics reserves it most glaring spotlight for the ice queens. Without Sonja Henie, it's conceivable that the rivalry between Nancy Kerrigan and Tonya Harding and the one between Michelle Kwan and Tara Lipinski might never have happened.

Sonja Henie changed the face of skating," said coach Frank Carroll, who trains Kwan. "According to anyone who saw her, she was the greatest of all time.

In an age when women sometimes were scolded for attempting jumps, Henie leaped with abandon. She was the first skater to integrate music and choreography into her programs. Her energy and creativity carried skating to a new level as a dynamic, entertaining sport.

"There is no question that Sonja Henie is the most important person—male or female—in skating history," said longtime coach Frank Carroll, who trains Kwan. "She not only made figure skating fashionable and entertaining, she really took it from nothing to something every woman wanted to do. There were little Sonja Henies running around everywhere."

Sonja Henie was the only woman to win three individual Olympic gold medals (1928, 1932, 1936) before parlaying her success on ice into a Hollywood career that rivaled those of Shirley Temple and Clark Gable in popularity.

Henie came out of Norway with flair and athleticism never before seen on ice. Because she came from a rich family, Henie was able to develop her skills through ballet lessons, private skating instructors, and the very best equipment money could buy. She traveled to all the top competitions well before she was a teenager.

What she brought to those competitions, along with a charming personality and youthful exuberance, was innovation. Before Henie, skating generally consisted of compulsories—tracings of figure eights and technical moves performed according to an acknowledged standard of execution. The emphasis was on discipline and mechanics, not artistic interpretation.

For Henie, artistry and athleticism was everything.

"Sonja Henie changed the face of skating," Carroll said. "According to anyone who saw her, she was the greatest of all time. She didn't care about barriers: she soared over them. She was so fast and athletic, she was in a class by herself."

In an age when women sometimes were scolded for attempting jumps, Henie leaped with abandon. She was the first skater to integrate music and choreography into her programs. Her energy and creativity carried skating to a new level as a dynamic, entertaining sport.

Then there was the look. No long skirts for Henie, as was the custom of the day. No black skates either. Henie replaced her modest costumes with something more appropriate for the late Roaring Twenties: short

Then there was the look. No long skirts for Henie as was the custom of the day. . . . No black skates either. Henie replaced her modest costumes with something more appropriate for the late Roaring Twenties: short skirts trimmed with fur and white boots. . . . Henie didn't intend on making a fashion statement. She simply wanted to be comfortable while jumping and spinning.

skirts trimmed with fur and white boots that shone as she skated across the ice.

Henie didn't intend on making a fashion statement. She simply wanted to be comfortable while jumping and spinning. But soon Henie realized that she could parlay her outfits, her style, and her gold medals into something more—superstardom.

"The ability to act and to skate was a unique and fantastic talent," said Carroll. "She was such an intelligent woman, and she knew how to turn her Olympic success into something much bigger."

In 1936, after her third straight Olympic crown—in addition to ten straight world titles—Henie turned professional and headed for America. Soon she was starring in touring ice shows that, for two decades, sold out regularly. And because she performed for as much as an hour in a two-hour show, Henie raised the bar on the physical demands of figure skating.

Then there was Hollywood. Henie's first film for Twentieth Century Fox, *One in a Million*, was a huge hit. She would star in nine more films that would earn an estimated $76 million at the box office.

A brilliant entrepreneur, Henie held stock in the New York Yankees and Madison Square Garden and owned a magnificent art collection. When she died in 1969, her estate was worth $47 million.

"If there was no Sonje Henie," says figure skating historian Dale Mitch, "there is no telling where skating might have headed."

After World War II, women's skating remained a major Olympic attraction, although not quite as spectacular as it was in Henie's day. North Americans dominated the sport after the war, with Canada's Barbara Ann Scott and America's Tenley Albright and Heiss leading the way. But it was not until Peggy Fleming's performance at the 1968 Olympics that figure skating became the premier sport for women.

Fleming was a shy nineteen-year-old whose elegance and commanding presence on ice was evident long before her arrival in Grenoble, France. She had won five U.S. and two world titles by then, the first

Peggy Fleming leaps high at the Olympic ice rink in preparation for her bid for a gold medal in the women's freestyle figure skating. Peggy was the only member of the U.S. team to win a gold medal at the 1968 Winter Olympics in Grenoble, France.

American champion to do so since the tragic 1961 plane crash that killed the entire U.S. team.

Thanks to the foresight of Roone Arledge, president of ABC Sports, the Grenoble Olympics were the first to be broadcast in color. And Arledge, knowing how Americans rally around their own during Olympic competition, one night devoted the network's prime time programming to Fleming's quest for the gold medal. Barring a catastrophe, Fleming already had the

gold medal clinched when she took the ice for the long program. Skating almost effortlessly to Tchaikovsky's *Sixth Symphony* in a chartreuse dress sewn by her mother, Fleming put on a magical display of grace and beauty.

"She was the 'Steel Ballerina,'" Carroll said. "She looked effortless but had an inner core of steel, and she would deliver every time. She looked like a butterfly."

America fell in love with her—and her sport.

The love affair with skating continued, thanks to an alluring young woman from East Germany, Katarina Witt. Rarely were skaters with such beauty and seductiveness seen on the ice.

Witt was eighteen when she burst upon the scene at the 1984 Sarajevo Olympics. Though she was not a great jumper or a particularly strong spinner, she could take a routine and, with a subtle facial expression or gesture, make it one that would linger in memory.

"I remember watching Katarina skate in Sarajevo," says Scott Hamilton, the men's gold medalist at those Olympics. "You felt as if she was looking every member of the audience—especially the men—right in the eye."

Witt repeated her gold medal performance in 1988 at the Calgary Olympics with a version of "Carmen" that one reviewer said "made mouths water." During her first news conference, the initial question from an American journalist was, "Will you marry me?"

While Witt was heating up the ice with her sultry artistic expression, a precocious youngster from the San Francisco suburbs was beginning her climb in American skating.

Kristi Yamaguchi became a champion in pairs before she ever reached the top in singles. She would have to

U.S. figure skater Kristi Yamaguchi performs her original program on the opening night of the women's figure skating event at the 1992 Winter Olympics in Albertville, France. Kristi won the gold medal for the U.S team at this event. *(left)*

Olympic women's figure skating champion Katarina Witt of East Germany mimics Michael Jackson as once again she captures the hearts of the audience at the 1988 Olympics in Calgary, Alberta. *(far left)*

end her partnership with Rudy Galindo before following Heiss, Fleming, and Dorothy Hamill and winning the 1992 Olympic crown.

Precision was Yamaguchi's calling card. Her spins were quick and tight, her footwork was exact, her jumps were perfect in form. In many ways, Yamaguchi was a textbook skater.

It wasn't until she turned professional and grew into one of the most elegant and versatile performers skating has seen that Yamaguchi really got her due. As a headliner on the Stars on Ice tour, she was the consummate entertainer, a perfect co-star with Hamilton.

Still, for all of the great women skaters and entertainers with their elegance, beauty and popularity, it took an incident straight from the pages of the tabloids or a soap opera to elevate figure skating to a level no other coed sport ever attained.

The rivalry between Nancy Kerrigan and Tonya Harding was a story that gripped the American television audience. Forget the cuteness and charm of Dorothy Hamill, the sexy mystery of Katarina Witt, or the precision of Kristi Yamaguchi. Nancy and Tonya had lifted figure skating from *The Wide World of Sports* to the worldwide evening news.

Tonya Harding and Nancy Kerrigan pose in January 1994 during the U.S. Figure Skating Championships in Detroit, Michigan. *(left)* Harding won the championship title once Kerrigan was unable to compete due to the injury sustained to her right knee when she was attacked by an assailant after a practice session.

Nancy Kerrigan performs one month later at the Winter Olympics in Lillehammer. *(right)* That Kerrigan, the heroine, skated superbly to win a silver medal, was uplifting. When Harding, the villain, fell all over the ice and finished eighth, it seemed a just reward for her treachery. Harding would later receive a lifetime ban from Olympic competition for planning the attack on Kerrigan, who retired after the Olympics.

"It was a negative event," said Carroll, who was plunked right into the middle of the story along with Kwan, "but it was the most positive thing that ever happened for women's sports. Ever."

Kerrigan and Harding were the top U.S. contenders at the 1994 Winter Olympics. A gold medal had meant millions to previous champions Witt and Yamaguchi, who went on to star in professional touring shows and became the darlings of sponsors and advertisers around the world.

At the time figure skating was already No. 2 for television ratings in the United States behind professional football. The Lillehammer Games, the first Winter Olympics held in a year when there was no Summer Olympics, would be a ratings bonanza for CBS. And the women figure skaters would be Lillehammer's biggest stars.

Little did anyone know just how big.

Thinking that an injury to the number one skater would clear his wife's path to Olympic gold—and further riches—Jeff Gillooly, Harding's husband, arranged to have Kerrigan attacked with a police baton as she left the practice rink at the national championships in Detroit. Kerrigan fell to the floor with a damaged knee, crying, "Why? Why?" Her reaction was captured by television cameras, and the tape quickly made its way to the evening news. Kerrigan was forced to withdraw from the event, which Harding won ahead of thirteen-year-old Michelle Kwan.

Kerrigan was given a medical bye and a spot on the Olympic team that the second-place finisher (Kwan) normally would have received. Kerrigan's place on the team was contingent on her passing a medical examination and skating at a training session observed by U.S. Olympic Committee and figure skating officials a month later. When she proved she was healthy enough to compete in Norway, Kerrigan was cleared to go.

By then, however, Harding's husband and his cohorts were at the center of the investigation into the attack. Day after day, the top story throughout the United States was the police probe into their involvement and what, if anything, Harding knew about the attack.

"You couldn't escape it," said Evy Scotvold, Kerrigan's coach. "We tried to keep Nancy as far away from all of it as possible, but the story was everywhere."

Once Harding's husband was arrested, the investigation shifted its focus to the skater. Would the USOC bar her from the Olympic team, particularly when Harding's representatives threatened a lawsuit? Would Harding confess to a role in the plot? Could Harding skate even moderately well if she *did* go to the Games?

The media were so entranced by the saga of Nancy and Tonya that camera crews staked out their homes and practice rinks. When the USOC backed down, allowing Harding to compete, the media circus descended on Lillehammer.

At their first practice together, in a tiny rink next to the competition venue, hundreds of print, radio, and television reporters crowded in, shoulder to shoulder. If you think Times Square on Millennium Eve was crowded . . . .

The ratings were, in a word, *Olympian*. On par with the Super Bowl and higher than any Olympic event in history.

That Kerrigan, the heroine, skated superbly to win a silver medal was uplifting. When Harding, the villain, fell all over the ice and finished eighth, it seemed a just reward for her treachery. Harding would later receive a lifetime ban from Olympic competition for planning the attack on Kerrigan, who retired after the Olympics. Harding did not appear in a professional event until 1999.

Figure skating benefitted bigtime from this incident. Made-for-TV competitions popped up everywhere and promoters scrambled to sign top

> Figure skating benefitted bigtime from this incident. Made-for-TV competitions popped up everywhere and promoters scrambled to sign top skaters for as many events as possible. Quality didn't matter, quantity did. . . . Yet people watched. They flocked to the arenas for competitions and ice shows. The strong television ratings led to huge rights fees, but the networks hardly flinched as they paid to present anything from the sensational Kwan vs. Lipinski showdowns to the nostalgic Witt vs. Baiul lovefests.

skaters for as many events as possible. Quality didn't matter, quantity did.

Yet people watched. They flocked to the arenas for competitions and ice shows. The strong television ratings led to huge rights fees, but the networks hardly flinched as they paid to present anything from the sensational Kwan vs. Lipinski showdowns to the nostalgic Witt vs. Baiul lovefests.

The Kwan-Lipinski rivalry was spectacular but short-lived. The sublime Kwan, two years older than Lipinski though still in her mid-teens, swept all of the major titles in 1996. But Lipinski surged past her the next year, becoming the youngest national and world champion at the age of fourteen.

Their timing was perfect: the Nagano Olympics were coming up. Where better to settle their duel than on the grandest of sports stages?

Michelle Kwan, silver medalist *(left)* **and Tara Lipinski**, gold medalist display their medals after the victory ceremony at the **1997 World Figure Skating Championships.**

Kwan had become a cover girl for the glamorous look she brought to the ice. Lipinski was more of a perky acrobat. Fans loved the contrast.

So did television, which played up the difference in the two skaters' personalities. When Kwan put forth a surpassing display of technique, artistry, and elegance in the national championships at Philadelphia—after overcoming a stress fracture in her foot, no less—and Lipinski rallied from a rough start to finish second, CBS could barely contain its glee.

It wasn't exactly Tonya-Nancy all over again, but it made for marvelous theater. Kwan, whose near-perfection in Philadelphia made her a favorite for Nagano, was portrayed as the new Fleming. Who could argue after Kwan had seven perfect 6.0s out of nine marks for presentation in the short program?

"When the 6.0s went up, I thought, 'Am I hearing this right?'" said Kwan. "Being in first, I couldn't have asked for more. I think it was one of my best short programs ever."

And she was even more untouchable in the free skate, when she earned eight more 6.0s for artistry, giving her fifteen, a record that might never be touched.

Lipinski, meanwhile, just kept on being her perky self. She posed for photos at Nagano with a

> Kwan had become a cover girl
>
> for the glamorous look she
>
> brought to the ice. Lipinski
>
> was more of a perky acrobat.
>
> Fans loved the contrast. . . .
>
> By the time the skating began,
>
> figure skating fans everywhere
>
> envisioned an Olympian battle.
>
> And they got it.

Michelle Kwan performs during her Exhibition Program at the 1999 World Figure Skating Championships.

sumo wrestler—"Beauty and the Beast," proclaimed one headline. She walked in the opening ceremonies while Kwan was at home practicing. She went to hockey games.

Lipinski was terrific in the short program, but Kwan was better. However, when Kwan let nerves and expectations affect her in the free skate, Lipinski jumped and twirled and danced right through the opening to win the gold medal.

"There is nothing that could be better for me," she said. "Anything that goes on in the future, I will be so content with what I have done."

Sadly, what Lipinski and Kwan had done in three years would have to stand for eternity. Lipinski, at fifteen the youngest Olympic champion ever, turned pro. Kwan remained eligible to compete in amateur competition, winning two more U.S. and world titles through the 2000 season and setting her sights on the 2002 Games in Salt Lake City. Their intense, thrilling rivalry had come to an end.

The names Michelle Kwan and Tara Lipinski are among the biggest in the sport today. As always, women are the main attraction in figure skating. That, at least, will never change.

Lipinski was terrific in the short program, but Kwan was better. However, when Kwan let nerves and expectations affect her in the free skate, Lipinski jumped and twirled and danced right through the opening to win the gold medal.

" When the 6.0s went up, I thought, 'Am I hearing this right?'" said Kwan. "Being in first, I couldn't have asked for more. I think it was one of my best short programs ever. "

The Other Miracle on Ice

*W*ake up, America! You have another miracle on ice. While you were sleeping, the U.S. women's team won the gold medal.

Sorry, but you missed an exciting game. There were gloves and sticks flying in the air, hugs and high-fives all around as these daring women inspired each other to win the gold.

How did it happen? How did the U.S. women defeat the Canadians, the preeminent power in women's hockey, to win the gold medal at the 1998 Nagano Olympics?

It all started for Cammi Granato ten years earlier, at the 1988 Olympics. At the opening ceremonies in Calgary, the sixteen-year-old watched as balloons soared high above the stadium and the athletes marched by. "I want to be an athlete. I have to be. If he can do this, I can too," Cammi said to her mom, who was seated beside her. "He" was her brother Tony, a member of the U.S. hockey team.

Like many of her teammates on the U.S. Olympic team, Granato, of Downers Grove, Illinois, grew up playing on boys' teams because there wasn't any organized hockey for girls in America. The state of Massachusetts was one exception, a true hockey stronghold for women, for it was there that U.S. Olympians Vicki Movsessian, Laurie Baker, Colleen Coyne, and Sandra Whyte learned how to play in organized women's leagues.

USA's Angela Ruggiero holds up an American flag following the gold medal win against Team Canada at the 1998 Nagano Olympics.

As it did for so many other girls, playing in boys' leagues enhanced Granato's skills. She was used to play-ing against the guys since she was a kid, tagging along with her three brothers to the rinks. Though she batted cleanup on a boys' baseball team and played basketball, soccer, and handball with the girls, Granato always returned to the sport of hockey.

When checking became a part of the game, Cammi had to rely on her wits and talent to outskate and outplay

87

the boys. Because she was the only girl on the ice, she was sometimes a target.

At one game, her coach overheard the opposition being told to "get number twenty-one," which was Cammi's number, so he devised a plan. Once Cammi had switched jerseys with a teammate who stood six feet tall, the rest of the game went smoothly. "When she was twelve or thirteen and started getting into checking [leagues], I started to worry a little," said Tony Granato, who went on to a solid NHL career. "Deep down, I was hoping she would play another sport."

Lisa Brown-Miller, a resident of Union Lake, Michigan, knows that kind of pressure.

"When I started playing [hockey] when I was six years old, my dad thought I was a little bit crazy; he thought it would be a passing phase," said Brown-Miller. "And, you know, here I am now, twenty-five years later, still playing."

Karen Bye changed her name to K.L. Bye on the team roster when she was fourteen just so she could play with the boys in River Falls, Wisconsin.

"It didn't bother me at all," she said. "In fact, I thought, 'Hey, this is kind of cool.' And the nickname stuck, too. To this day, I'm 'K.L.' in the dressing room."

Bye wasn't alone. Women did whatever was necessary to play hockey. Although women had been playing the sport for most of the century, it wasn't until the 1990s that women's hockey caught the world's attention.

The first World Championship for women was

held in 1990. Canada beat the United States, then beat the Americans again in 1992, 1994, and 1997. The Canadians were the favorites at the '98 Olympics, the first year that women's hockey became a medal sport at the Games. Although Canada and the United States were considered the top two teams, Canada had more tradition, better arenas to practice and play in, and, usually, better players.

The Americans' advancement in the sport took a quantum leap from 1990 to 1997, when the number of females registered in USA Hockey programs quadrupled to reach 23,000. Before the '90s, there were less than 100 women playing hockey in America's high school programs. By 1999, there were more than 3,500. In 1994, Minnesota became the first state to sanction women's hockey for high school teams. And colleges, aided by the groundbreaking Title IX legislation, added varsity programs to go along with the traditional club teams that had been in existence since the '70s.

Although Canada beat the United States 8-0 in the '92 world championship, the Americans appeared to be catching up. In 1997, they took the Canadians into overtime before losing 4-3. In thirteen exhibition games prior to the '98 Olympics, the American women won six.

Playing in the Olympics was a long-term commitment. If the American team was to succeed, its women would have to put their lives on hold for two years. Brown-Miller, postponing her honeymoon, headed to training camp the day after her wedding. She had already quit her job as coach at Princeton. Sarah Tueting, one of the U.S. goaltenders, postponed her study of neurobiology at Dartmouth. The entire team made sacrifices so they could perform at their very best in the inaugural Olympic competition.

"You can't turn down an opportunity like that," said Tueting of Winnetka, Illinois. Like many younger sisters, Tueting started tagging along with her brother Jonathan to his hockey

> **I don't think Sarah playing hockey particularly fit the Winnetka image of what a young girl ought to be doing,"** her father said. **"But we never asked anyone to make allowances for Sarah, and no one ever did.**

U.S. player Jennifer Schmidgall (*left*) falls down on Team Canada player Therese Brisson in first period action.

games. At one of his games, Sarah kept moving from one end of the rink to the other, fascinated by one goal-tender in particular.

"My parents thought I had a crush," she said. Actually, she was only studying his moves. Tueting liked hanging around the guys, but it had nothing to do with dating. "Sarah went after hockey a lot because of her older brother and also because at an early age she decided boys had more fun," said her father.

The perils of goaltending didn't faze Tueting. She shrugged off stitches to her head as part of the job. "I don't think Sarah playing hockey particularly fit the Winnetka image of what a young girl ought to be doing," her father said. "But we never asked anyone to make allowances for Sarah, and no one ever did." This attitude helped Sarah and her high school boy's team win the state championship when she was a senior.

At Dartmouth, Tueting became disenchanted with women's hockey. "The transition from men's hockey to women's hockey was tough," Tueting said. "It wasn't fun. I used to get real [mad] after a loss, and I was about the only one."

So, when the call came from Ben Smith, coach of the U.S. women's national team, to try out for the

Olympic squad, she headed for camp with renewed enthusiasm. "Now I was playing for the love of the game," she said. She didn't know she made the team until December 20, less than two months before the Olympics would begin. Along with Sara DeCosta, Tueting would be one of two goalies on the twenty-player U.S. squad. Both were relatively inexperienced at the international level compared to Canada's goal-tending corps, which included Manon Rheaume, the first woman to play in the NHL.

"That's a huge advantage for us, going into the Olympic games," said Canadian coach Shannon Miller. "They have two rookies who have little or no experience other than exhibition games at this level."

Tueting wasn't intimidated. "A puck's a puck," she said.

The rivalry between the Americans and Canadians intensified during their thirteen-game, four-month pre-Olympic tour across North America. Every game was fiercely competitive and emotional. Miller was so upset following a 3-0 loss to the Americans in the final of the Three Nations Cup on December 20 that she banned her players from drinking alcohol over the Christmas holidays.

As expected, both teams advanced to the gold medal game at Nagano.

"Canada's always had the edge . . . but throughout the tournament we gained confidence," DeCosta said. "We played them so many times, got to know them so well, we knew we could beat them."

A preliminary-round game was a huge confidence builder for the Americans. They rallied from a 4-1 deficit in the third period to beat the Canadians 7-4 in a physical, penalty-filled contest.

Both Tueting and DeCosta had played well during the pre-Olympic tour and in the preliminary rounds. Coach Smith had a tough choice picking his starter for the gold medal game.

"Sarah Tueting wants the ball, and she does better when she's in there from the start," said Smith, giving Tueting the nod in goal. Talk about pressure!

Unable to sleep the night before the big game, Sarah paced around her room. Though it was late, she still had too much energy, so she picked up an apple and let it fly across the room until it landed with a loud *thud* against the wall. She reached into the bowl and picked up another and another, hurling each apple harder than the one before. "Get away from me!" cried her room-

mate. Having emptied the bowl of fruit, Sarah finally settled down and went to sleep.

The next day, Sarah went to work. Tueting and Rheaume were both strong in the first period and the two sides headed into the dressing room after twenty minutes locked in a scoreless tie. The Americans

Canada's always had the edge . . . but throughout the tournament we gained confidence," DeCosta said. "We played them so many times, got to know them so well, we knew we could beat them.

Jennifer Schmidgall (left) rejoices after the U.S. scored a goal less than three minutes into the second period, adding another to make the score 2-0 in the third period of the gold medal game. Then, with just four minutes remaining, the Canadians regrouped to cut the margin to 2-1. Canada's goalie Manon Rheaume (right) and team-mate Therese Brisson (center) still hope for a comeback.

scored less than three minutes into the second period, adding another goal to make the score 2-0 in the third. Then, with just four minutes remaining, the Canadians cut the margin to 2-1. There was still hope for a comeback.

With little more than a minute left and the Canadians pressing hard, Tueting made a kick-save to clear the puck from goal. The Canadians, desperately needing to send the game into overtime, pulled Rheaume for an extra attacker. But the Americans quickly dashed their hopes by scoring into an empty net. The victory was theirs.

Sarah Tueting *(foreground)* **waves to cheering fans along with her teammates after their gold medal victory over Team Canada at the 1998 Nagano Olympics.**

Cammi Granato *(left)* and K.L. Bye show their gold medals during the medals ceremony.

It was bedlam. The American bench emptied to join their victorious teammates on the ice. Players hugged each other as they wept and smiled.

"I saw flowers," Bye said. "I saw hands in the air."

Many of the euphoric American women looked to the stands for family members, hoping to share the glorious experience with their loved ones. The sweat-soaked Tueting spotted her mom and dad. "They were jumping around," recalls Tueting. "It's probably the happiest I've seen my mom." Tueting had been carrying a coin blessed by a monk for good luck. It was given to her by her brother Jonathan. Later she wore a red, white, and blue-striped Uncle Sam hat—another present from Jonathan—and carried a bouquet of flowers.

Engulfed in all the excitement, it would take time before the American women could comprehend the scope of their accomplishment. Perhaps that would come in quiet moments away from the media and the screaming fans who greeted them after their victory.

The American women had won the first Olympic gold medal for women's hockey. But that was not all. They became the focus of worldwide attention and sparked new interest in the sport of hockey—for both men and women. A professional women's hockey league was now possible.

Miller, the Canadian coach, took the loss bitterly.

> It's a nice reward for all those obstacles—all people told us was we don't belong out there," said Granato, " . . . that women shouldn't play a men's game.

93

OLYMPIC CHAMPION
Manon Rheaume ★ Goalie

Exhibition games in the NHL usually don't create too much excitement. Yet there was a buzz when the Tampa Bay Lightning stepped on the ice to meet the St. Louis Blues on September 23, 1992. Why all the commotion? A young woman—yes, a woman—was starting in goal for the Lightning.

Manon Rheaume was accustomed to breaking barriers, having been the first woman to play in the Quebec Major Junior Hockey League. Lightning general manager Phil Esposito, an NHL Hall of Famer, invited Rheaume to the Tampa Bay training camp in the fall of '92. While hoping to gain some publicity for his expansion team, Esposito also felt that Rheaume was good enough to play men's professional hockey.

When Rheaume led the Lightning onto the ice, the crowd gave her a standing ovation. Forty seconds into the game, she stopped her first shot. But within moments a thirty-five-foot slap shot hit Rheaume's pads and, before she could react, the puck went between her legs and into the net. "It was a bad goal," Rheaume admitted, "but even good NHL goalies give up bad goals."

Rheaume soon had a chance to redeem herself. The Blues were on a power play when Ron Sutter laid a crossing pass on Nelson Emerson's stick. The wide-open Emerson had Rheaume at his mercy. He fired a wrist shot into the upper right side of the goal. Rheaume reacted quickly, sliding across the goalmouth to snare the shot with her glove. The crowd went wild! The Lightning, led by Rheaume's brilliant defense, had killed the power play. Rheaume later gave up a goal on a sizzling low shot to her stick side before leaving with the score tied at two after one period. The Lightning eventually lost 6-4.

Rheaume proved her mettle as a player for professional teams in Atlanta, Knoxville, Nashville, and Reno, often facing prejudice from her teammates in the minor leagues.

Rheaume, who played for Canada's world championship team in 1992, came back to compete in the 1998 Olympics at Nagano. Despite a strong performance, she had to settle for the silver medal when Canada was beaten in a close game by the United States. Rheaume vowed to try again for the gold at Salt Lake City.

"When you have a dream, you want to go after that dream," she said.

" When you have a dream," she said, " you want to go after that dream. "

Manon Rheaume makes her 1992 debut with the NHL as goalie for the Tampa Bay Lightning. *(above)*

Team Canada goalie, Rheaume watches as the USA team celebrates its 3-1 victory over Canada during the 1998 Nagano Olympics.

Her feelings changed, however, once she attended the medal ceremonies. "I had a feeling of joy go through my body because I realized an Olympic gold medal was being hung on a female hockey player," she said. "I couldn't believe the impact it had on me."

The U.S. women winning the gold brought back memories of 1980, when the American men shocked the world by upsetting the mighty Soviet team and winning the gold medal at Lake Placid. While the victory at Nagano was not quite as dramatic, it did put the U.S. women—and their sport—on the international sports map.

Playing games in her basement with her brothers, Granato had pretended to be Mike Eruzione, who scored the winning goal against the Soviets. Now there was no more make believe, no more dreaming about Olympic ice.

"It's a nice reward for all those obstacles—all people told us was we don't belong out there, that women shouldn't play a men's game," she said.

The new Olympic champions had their own miracle to celebrate.

> **I had a feeling of joy go through my body because I realized an Olympic gold medal was being hung on a female hockey player,"**
>
> **Coach Miller said. "I couldn't believe the impact it had on me.**

"*i* don't know how you can beat that. To do something you love and get paid for it," said Gloria Cordes Elliot, "there's nothing better."

Diamond Darlings

*i*t was win or go home for the Kalamazoo Lassies when, in the bottom of the ninth, Gloria Cordes stood on the mound, the ball in her hand and the entire season on her shoulders.

The scene was the 1954 playoffs for the All-American Girls Professional Baseball League. The Lassies trailed the powerhouse Fort Wayne Daisies two games to one in a best-of-five series that would deter-mine the league champion. The Lassies were only three outs away from victory and a chance to play a decisive Game 5. But first Cordes would have to face the three best hitters in the Daisies' line-up.

The Lassies had scored four times in the top of the eighth inning to take a 6-5 lead, and that's the way the score stood with the Daisies batting in the bottom of the ninth.

When Cordes gave up a single to Kate Horstman, the crowd of 1,613 cheered in anticipation of a rally.

The next batter bunted, moving Horstman to second on the sacrifice.

Home run threat Jo Weaver was up next. The Lassies' manager signaled for the intentional walk.

Now there were runners on first and second with one out. A ground ball could help the Lassies win the game with a doubleplay. Coming up were Betty Foss and Jean Geissinger, the top two hitters in the league. This was the moment of truth for both Cordes and the Kalamazoo Lassies.

Cordes looked in for the sign. Both her curveball and her stinging fastball were working that day. No problem, she thought.

Pitching from the stretch, she fired to Foss, who popped to short. Next up was the ever dangerous Geissinger.

Strikeout!

The Kalamazoo Lassies lived to play another day. They finished the season in grand style by winning the championship, the last team to do so before the league folded after the 1954 season.

"The league decided maybe it would be a good idea to take a year off and find new cities," said Gloria Elliott, who has married since her days on the baseball diamond. "But it just never got back. We took that year off and that was the end of it. We all thought we'd be coming back in another year."

DIAMOND DARLING
Toni Stone ★ Negro Baseball League

It was the 1940s and, like many young athletes in America, Toni Stone dreamed of playing baseball in the major leagues.

There was a problem—actually, two: Toni was black and she was a woman.

Though she never made it to the majors, she did make history. After Jackie Robinson broke the color line in baseball, Stone broke the gender line in the Negro Leagues.

Like Robinson, Stone endured indignities and taunts, even from her own teammates. But she kept fighting to prove she belonged. And prove it she did.

Playing with a succession of black men's professional teams, she finally arrived at the top level of the Negro Leagues in the early '50s, which featured the finest black baseball talent in America. Through its ranks came such future major league stars as Robinson, Roy Campanella, Satchel Paige, and Hank Aaron. In fact, Stone replaced Aaron at second base for the Indianapolis Clowns.

Replacing the great Hank Aaron was one thing. Winning acceptance was entirely another matter. Stone was the only female in an all-male world at a time when it was considered unthinkable—even outrageous—for a woman to play baseball in a men's league. Her manager and teammates resented her. Some believed she was only playing because many top players had left the Negro Leagues for the majors. They thought she was a sideshow to bring in crowds. But Stone played in fifty games, most of them non-league exhibitions, and batted a respectable .243.

Few players—men or women—were more resilient or tougher than Stone. An incident experienced during her time with the Kansas City Monarchs sums up everything about Stone as a player.

With a man on first, she was playing second near the outfield grass, hoping to turn a double play. The ball was hit to third baseman Ralph Johnson, who turned and fired a high throw to Stone, who was crossing the bag. The ball tipped off Stone's glove, hitting her head.

She collapsed in the dirt, unconscious. She lay flat on the ground, not moving a muscle, as frightened players rushed to her aid.

"I was scared because it took about three or four minutes before we could revive her," Johnson remembered.

No problem.

"She got up, brushed off her pants, and got right back out there and started playing again."

DIAMOND DARLING
Mamie "Peanuts" Johnson ★ Negro Baseball League

Mamie "Peanuts" Johnson spent hot, dusty summer days playing pickup baseball as a child in the 1940s and dreamed of making the big leagues. Johnson overcame rejection by the all-white women's league that began playing during World War II and became one of only three women to play in the Negro leagues. As a pitcher for the Indianapolis Clowns from 1953-1955,

Johnson compiled a record of thirty-three wins against eight losses. "Everything about my time playing professional baseball was beautiful," Johnson said. "And being a pitcher, it was a tremendous joy to strike some of the fellows out. Because they thought that by me being a girl, this was something of a joke, but it wasn't a joke and I had to let them know that. That was the joy."

Washed up at the age of twenty-two. That was one way of looking at it. But Elliott had memories from her five years in the league that would last her a lifetime.

"I don't know how you can beat that. To do something you love and get paid for it, there's nothing better."

Ask any of the 545 women who played in the AAGPBL during its twelve years of existence and you would no doubt get the same response.

The league, founded by Chicago Cubs owner P.K. Wrigley in 1943, might not have formed if not for World War II. Fearful that the drafting of major league players might shut down professional baseball, Wrigley looked for an alternative to fill the stadiums.

In a scene from the film *A League of Their Own*, starring Madonna, Rosie O'Donnell and Geena Davis, Jon Lovitz plays the role of a scout who recruits two sisters from a farm for the new women's baseball league. Real life wasn't much different from reel life, as scouts searched every corner of America to find female talent.

The major leagues somehow managed to survive the war years, as did the women's league. It lasted beyond the war, proving that women's baseball was more than just a novelty or a substitute. Based in the Midwest and playing mostly in small makeshift stadiums and high school fields, the ten teams in the AAGPBL drew as many as a million spectators in 1948.

Gloria Cordes grew up on Staten Island, New York, with five sports-minded brothers. In the summer of 1949, she played with a Police Athletic League girls softball team—the same year two touring teams from the AAGPBL came to town for an exhibition game.

She and her friends attended the game—and, for Gloria, it turned out to be more than just another pleasant summer evening watching baseball.

"They announced they were having tryouts before the game," she recalled about that fateful night.

Gloria jumped at the chance. A couple of tryouts later, she was wearing the uniform of the Muskegon Lassies, later to become the Kalamazoo Lassies. By her third year in the league she was making the maximum under the salary cap—$100 a week. (By comparison, she had been making $30 a week working for an insurance company in Manhattan). She also played in Racine, Wisconsin, and Battle Creek, Michigan, before finishing up at Kalamazoo.

"They just traded you where you were needed to keep the league more or less even and have good games," she said.

During her time in the league, Gloria Cordes was regarded as one of its top pitchers. Her best season was her third. She started and finished twenty-four games, posted a 1.44 earned run average and a 16-8 record for a fifth-place team.

When the league broke up, it broke many hearts.

"I was just getting into it and I was really young," Elliott recalled. "Life goes on, but it was sad, and the worst part was I had to work for my money now."

Ila Borders ★ Pitcher

Ila Borders was ten when baseball became an important part of her life. She wanted to be a pitcher. Her father, a former minor league player, fully supported her. "He said, 'If you really want to do it, let's go to work,'" Borders recalls.

Growing up, Borders had to deal with prejudice. When she played Little League in southern California, boys tossed rocks at her. Things only grew worse as she moved from high school to college ball. Borders played on two men's teams and described the experience as "hell on earth." Teammates threw balls, and sometimes bats, at her face.

Fast forward to the pros, where the left-handed Borders made her professional debut on May 31, 1997. It was not with the Silver Bullets, the all-girls baseball team, but with the St. Paul Saints. This was in the Northern League, where Darryl Strawberry began his notorious comeback to the majors. She came on in relief but failed to get a batter out. The next day was different. She got the job done, retiring the side.

"My first year was nothing but survival," said Borders. Her second year was more about "getting established."

Staying in the Northern League, she pitched for the Duluth-Superior Dukes in her second year and then the Madison Black Wolf in her third, making an impression at both stops. At Duluth, the 5-foot-10, 150-pound Borders became the first woman to start a minor league game, allowing three runs in five innings en route to an 8-3 loss to Sioux Falls.

"If all our starters could keep teams at three runs for five innings, we'd probably be doing a lot better," said Dukes manager George Mitterwald. "She did an outstanding job."

The next time out, the southpaw with the ponytail shut out the Sioux Falls Canaries for six innings. Again, a first. Next, she became the first woman to win a game in professional baseball. Borders, whose performances had increased attendance around the league, proved to be more than just a sideshow.

"It was a close, low-scoring game, when the team was fighting for first place," she said of her win over Sioux Falls. "They couldn't accuse me of just being a mop-up pitcher after that."

Hardly. At Madison, Borders became an effective starter thanks to a unique pitching system by manager "Dirty Al" Gallagher. Borders was used only as a three-inning starter, that way hitters usually got only one look at her and didn't have time to adjust to her repertoire.

Under Gallagher's system, Borders finished the 1999 season with a sparkling 1.53 earned run average and held opposing batters to a composite .254 batting average.

"She has good movement [on her pitches] and throws a nice, little screwball," Gallagher said. "She has great control. The problem is she doesn't throw hard enough. She's not a big person. If she were 6-foot-1, 190 pounds, I have no reservations that she would go to the majors."

Borders has an eighty mile per hour fastball. Most major leaguers throw in the nineties.

Even so, she hasn't thrown in the towel.

"Everybody tells me I don't belong out there, Borders said. "Sometimes it gets to me, but no one's going to run me off."

> "My first year was nothing but survival," said Borders. Her second year was more about 'getting established.' "Everybody tells me I don't belong out there. Sometimes it gets to me, but no one's going to run me off."

Ila Borders made history on a Saturday night, May 31, 1997, as she made her pitching debut for the St. Paul Saints against the Sioux Falls Canaries in Sioux Falls, South Dakota. She became the first woman to pitch in a men's regular season professional game.

" Women should have every opportunity to play competitive professional ball," said Phil Neikro, Silver Bullets manager and former Atlanta Braves pitcher. "I think we are going to surprise quite a few people with the ability of these athletes and the caliber of ball they can play. "

Silver Bullets pitcher Pam Davis doffs her cap for the National Anthem before an exhibition game in 1996 between the Jacksonville Suns and the Australian Olympic team. *(right)*

Silver Bullets ★ Women's Professional Baseball Team

It was a dream that lasted for five seasons, and it proved beyond a shadow of a doubt that women could play professional baseball. The Silver Bullets, sponsored by the Coors Brewing Company in Colorado, were the only all-female professional baseball team to be officially recognized by the National Association of Professional Baseball Leagues and Major League Baseball. When the formation of the team was announced in December 1993 and tryouts were held shortly thereafter, women from all walks of life put their careers on hold for the chance to play professional baseball.

Hall of Famer and ace knuckleball pitcher Phil Niekro was the overwhelming choice as the team's manager. "Women should have every opportunity to play competitive professional ball," he said. "I think we are going to surprise quite a few people with the ability of these athletes and the caliber of ball they can play."

Among the players who made the team were Julie Croteau, first base, who was the first woman to play NCAA baseball and, later, the first woman to coach baseball at that level. Joining her on the diamond were Pam Davis, a former USF softball pitcher who, like many of the other candidates, was making the transition from the slower paced game of softball to baseball, with its off-speed pitches, such as curveballs and sliders, and hard hitting.

At first the Silver Bullets were something of a novelty item as they embarked on a fifty-game season against teams composed of men's minor-league, semipro, and amateur teams. But that impression began to change once they got a couple of seasons under their belts. "We just need experience," Niekro insisted. "That's all we need to get better."

In each successive season, the Silver Bullets improved their play as a team as well as their record. They became competitive in a game that had been played for years by their opponents, but which was, for many of the women on the team, still fairly new.

"The Silver Bullets help accomplish three things," said outfielder Angie Marzetta. "One, they give women a chance to compete. Two, they provide an opportunity beyond college for women to pursue baseball. Three, they show that women should be able to play most of the same sports as men."

By the end of the 1998 season, The Silver Bullets accomplished all they had set out to achieve, compiling their first winning record of 23-22. Unfortunately, Coors, citing changes in sponsorship sales, withdrew their support of the team and the Silver Bullets were forced to disband.

Silver Bullets manager and former Atlanta Braves pitcher Phil Niekro watches over practice on the first day of spring training in 1996.

chapter nine

"I take pride in thinking that I might have made it easier for anyone coming in," Muldowney said. "...especially the ladies, and I think I did.*"*

First Ladies

*t*hree women in a hurry. They didn't start out to break the gender barrier, they only wanted to arrive at the finish line first. In the end, Shirley Muldowney, Janet Guthrie, and Julie Krone accomplished both.

As the first female drag race driver, Shirley Muldowney crashed through stereotypes and proved that women could compete in what was once considered a strictly all-male sport. And along came Janet Guthrie in open-wheel auto racing and Julie Krone in horse racing to knock down barriers in those sports.

Muldowney was the first woman licensed by the National Hot Rod Association (NHRA) to drive Top Fuel dragsters, the fastest race cars in the world. She won a record-tying three NHRA titles competing against the top male drivers in the world, not to mention eighteen national events and a Driver of the Year award.

Guthrie was the first woman to compete in the Indianapolis 500 and, in a rare venture into stock cars, the only woman to compete in the Daytona 500. Krone was the first female jockey to win 2,000 races, with 1,500 more to come, and she was the first and only woman to win a Triple Crown race.

They're off!

Shirley Muldowney is all smiles after just completing a qualifying run at 250.69 mph in the U.S. Nationals drag races. That tied the track and event speed records. Muldowney vied to become the first woman to win the U.S. Nationals August 31, 1979.

At the age of sixteen, Shirley married Jack Muldowney. It was a marriage made in drag-strip heaven. Both Jack and Shirley loved fast cars. Jack, a top auto mechanic, kept building her cars, each faster than the one before. . . . She was soon driving "an eleven-second car,". . . .Then there was the other vehicle she drove. Women weren't supposed to be able to handle Funny Cars, particularly a woman the size of the 5-foot-4 Muldowney. Yet she won a Funny Car title in North Carolina. In 1971 she moved to Michigan. Shirley was going to be a dragster.

"I'm lucky to be alive today, not from racing—from the rides we took on the street."

Shirley "Cha Cha" Muldowney was only fifteen and already in the fast lane.

"I would drive anything I could get my hands on," said Muldowney.

"I raced the cars I drove to work."

While Muldowney's passion for speed thrilled her, it frightened her mother. Her daughter had been racing up and down the roads of Schenectady, New York, and Mae Roque was worried that Shirley was getting mixed up with the wrong crowd.

"They were having fun, but it was a dangerous game, too."

At the age of sixteen, Shirley married Jack Muldowney. It was a marriage made in drag-strip heaven.

Both Jack and Shirley loved fast cars. Jack, a top auto mechanic, kept building her cars, each faster than the one before. She started at small tracks in upstate New York and quickly graduated to bigger speedways and faster cars. She was soon driving "an eleven-second car," meaning it could travel a quarter mile in eleven seconds.

> " I think the women's liberation movement was an advantage for me," Muldowney said. "The fact that I was a woman in racing helped the media take notice. "

Then there was the other vehicle she drove. Down the track would come this strange-looking car. Unsteady as it rode along, it would jerk violently until it came to a stop. Unexpectedly, out would come a young lady with a broad smile.

Was this a circus act? No, it was Shirley Muldowney competing in the Funny Car, a car that had a shorter wheel base than the classic drag racing cars, a full body, and an engine in front instead of behind the driver.

Women weren't supposed to be able handle Funny Cars, particularly a woman the size of the 5-foot-4 Muldowney. Yet she won a Funny Car title in Rockingham, North Carolina. In 1971, she moved to Michigan to put her national career into high gear.

Shirley Muldowney was going to be a dragster.

The male-dominated NHRA had other ideas. Getting a license to race in the dangerous Top Fuel category was a two-year battle for Muldowney. She continually met opposition, even while racing at dazzling speeds that matched, and sometimes surpassed, those of the men. But Muldowney continued to believe. As her victories mounted, the NHRA had no choice but to concede to her demands to join the circuit. At first it was easier winning acceptance from her fellow drivers than from drag racing fans.

"Of course it was because I was a woman," she says. "The spectators really took it to heart if I put their favorite, like Big Daddy Don Garlits, away."

Once Muldowney started winning races, she began developing a following of her own. Her first national victory in Top Fuel came in 1976 in Columbus, Ohio. "I think the women's liberation movement was an advantage for me," Muldowney said. "The fact that I was a woman

Shirley Muldowney takes off in a cloud of smoke during a qualifying run for the 14th annual NHRA Internationals at Pomona Raceway in Pomona, California. Shirley, who entered in the Top Fuel Eliminator class, was the only female entrant in the competition.

Then her world suddenly came crashing down . . . Muldowney was driving in a qualifying run for a race in St. Pie, Quebec, in the summer of 1984 when, suddenly, she saw black strips of rubber peeling off of her left front tire. Instead of flying harmlessly into the air, the black snakes of rubber wound themselves tightly around her front wheel.

in racing helped the media take notice."

Who couldn't help but notice? The perky Muldowney was hard to miss, roaring down the straightaway at well over 200 miles an hour in a pink 1,800-pound, 3,500-horsepower vehicle. In 1977, she became only the second driver to shatter the 250-mph barrier, and won the first of her three NHRA world titles that year. She also won in 1980 and 1982. And in 1981, she was the American Hot Rod Association champ, making it four world titles in six years. It didn't look like she could be stopped.

Then her world suddenly came crashing down.

Muldowney was driving in a qualifying run for a race in St. Pie, Quebec, in the summer of 1984 when, suddenly, she saw black strips of rubber peeling off of her left front tire. Instead of flying harmlessly into the air, the black snakes of rubber wound themselves tightly around her front wheel. Her knuckles turning white, she held the steering wheel in a death grip as her vehicle careened off the road at nearly 250 miles an hour. Flying over a ten-foot gully, the dragster dropped straight down and disintegrated as it hit an embankment. Muldowney was rushed to a Montreal hospital, where she remained in the intensive care unit for two months.

Yet, several operations and nineteen months later, Muldowney was back behind the wheel. She literally could not cross her legs when she sat down and had to walk with a crutch, but she could sit in a dragster and hit the pedal.

"I love racing so much," she said, "I just had to come back."

Her love of drag racing was so great that she continued to race late into her fifties despite being

driven off the NHRA track by high costs and a lack of sponsorship. Muldowney, now divorced from her first husband and remarried to longtime crew chief Rahn Tobler, turned to the lower-profile International Hod Rod Association (IHRA) and barnstorming for steady work.

She wasn't just there for the show. In one stretch during 1996, she appeared in five consecutive IHRA races, winning three and finishing second in total points. In 1998, she set IHRA records for elapsed time (4.696 seconds) and speed (312.50 mph) while covering a quarter-mile.

Muldowney opened doors for women like Cristen Powell, Angelle Seeling, Stephanie Reaves and Shelly Anderson to make their mark in drag racing.

"I take pride in thinking that I might have made it easier for anyone coming in, especially the ladies, and I think I did," Muldowney said.

Does a woman have enough strength to drive a race car for 500 miles? Janet Guthrie answers the question this way: "I drive the car, I don't carry it."

She was thirty-nine when she made racing history in 1977 as the first woman to compete in the Indy 500, though mechanical problems kept her from completing the race. She made up for it in 1978 when she finished ninth in a field of thirty-three. Driving with a broken right wrist which she kept a secret, she hit speeds approaching 200 miles per hour.

Breaking the Indy gender barrier wasn't the only reason Guthrie's driving suit and helmet found a place in the Smithsonian. As one of the top drivers in her sport, she is in the Women's Sports Hall of Fame and listed in Who's Who in the World.

With dirt-and-oil grimed face, Janet Guthrie, the first woman to ever drive in the World 600 stock car race, steps from her racer on Sunday, May 31, 1976, after driving the full 600 miles and finishing in fifteenth positon. *(above)*

Guthrie had the right stuff, that's for sure. At first, she was going to be an astronaut—or, at the very least, a pilot—before she applied it to auto racing.

As a sixteen-year-old, she convinced her father, a pilot, that she could make a free-fall parachute jump. How? By jumping off the roof of her Miami, Florida, home and landing safely.

"I decided to show him that I could jump off a roof without harm," Guthrie said.

Then her father took her up for a real jump. She landed without injury, but her father refused to do it again. "He said that it was too hard on him."

Think of how he must have felt when Janet enrolled in NASA's astronaut program. By then she had already earned a degree in physics at the University of Michigan and worked as an aeronautical engineer, in addition to earning a commercial pilot's license. She survived the first round of the astronaut program, one of only four women who did. She didn't get past the second, however.

"I have an interest in seeing what's out there at the boundaries of human experience," said Guthrie, explaining her passion for new challenges.

Another one of Guthrie's passions is cars. In 1963, she bought a Jaguar XK140 that was designed for racing. She was hooked and began competing. Despite her failure to find a sponsor, Guthrie found a way. She set up a makeshift garage in the back of her station wagon, which she also used as her sleeping quarters. She didn't have enough money for both car parts and hotels.

"I could always use the track restroom to get all spiffed up and go out to dinner at a fancy restaurant," she said. "Then I'd come back and get in my sleeping bag in the station wagon."

After ten years of low profile driving, she quit her regular job to go full-blast into racing. "I knew it was going to take a lot out of my life, and it did," she said. "It demanded every resource I had, financially and psychologically."

Guthrie won the North Atlantic Road Racing championship in 1973, but by 1975 her draining lifestyle was finally taking its toll. She was ready to quit. Then the Indianapolis car builder Rolla Vollstedt gave Guthrie the break she had been looking for when he invited her to test his car for a possible run at the Indianapolis Motor Speedway. After driving in her first oval-track race in 1976, she was ready for the biggest test of her life.

Guthrie won the North Atlantic Road Racing championship in 1973, but by 1975 her draining lifestyle was finally taking its toll. She was ready to quit. Then Rolla Vollstedt gave Guthrie the break she had been looking for when he invited her to test his car for a possible run at the Indianapolis Motor Speedway. After driving in her first oval-track race in 1976, she was ready for the biggest test of her life.

"Photographers were everywhere," she recalls of that first chance to race at world famous Indy. "We knew there would be a flurry in the newspapers about a woman at the Indy track, but we were all astonished by the commotion it caused."

Even though he got "a lot of flak" from the male drivers on the racing circuit, Vollestedt showed courage in bringing Guthrie to Indy as a driver. For most of the track's history, women were persona non grata. It was not until 1971 that they were allowed in the pits.

Guthrie was less than well received by the media. Reporters said women didn't have the strength, endurance, or emotional stability to race. Some in the track crowd were even rougher on Guthrie. "We hope you crash right in front of our corner," one male fan shouted at her.

The hostility didn't keep her from passing her rookie test that day. One year later, she qualified for the Indy 500 with the fastest time on the second weekend of qualifying.

"The fact that I set a woman's record in the process, I really didn't care about," Guthrie said. "The important thing to me was qualifying well for a race that was the top level of competition in the United States."

It wasn't long before Guthrie began earning the respect of other drivers, as well as the fans, particularly after her high finish in the 1978 Indy 500. All told, she competed in eleven Indy races. Some of her other accomplishments include being the only woman to have competed in the Daytona 500, where she won top rookie honors in 1977, and a fifth place finish at the Bettenhausen 200 in Milwaukee. At the 1977 Talladega 500, Guthrie's qualifying time was fastest in the field, beating Richard Petty, Bobby Allison, and Johnny Rutherford.

Guthrie walked away from racing in 1986, disappointed because, despite her accomplishments, she still had difficulty getting sponsors. She was saddened, too, that not many women had followed her into the sport. But in her time Guthrie showed racing's good 'ol boys a thing or two.

Janet Guthrie puts on her fire-resistant gloves before heading out on the Daytona Speedway course on July 2, 1976, in preparation for the Firecracker 400 race which was run on Independence Day.

Jockey Julie Krone *(right)* rides Life Boat in the eighth race at Belmont Park in Elmont, N.Y., May 25, 1994. It was Krone's first mount since she was seriously injured in a spill at Saratoga on August 30, 1993. In that accident Krone suffered a bruised heart that could have killed her, a puncture on the inside of her elbow, and a shattered right ankle.

Just turned thirty, Krone hoped to add more numbers to her already impressive accomplishments: 2,762 wins in nearly 16,000 races, totaling almost $54 million in earnings. In 1993 she rode Colonial Affair to win the Belmont Stakes, thus becoming the first woman to win a Triple Crown event.

The 4-foot-10, 100-pound Krone urged her 1,000-pound mount into the wall of thundering horses. Shoulder to shoulder with her fellow jockeys, dirt covering the sweat on her face, she took Seattle Way on a thrilling, gritty ride. She came off the backstretch, rounded the turn, and was headed for home and certain victory when the unexpected happened.

One of the jockeys steered his horse into Krone's path. Her horse's knees buckled, throwing Krone from the saddle. A crippling pain wracked her body as she landed heavily on her right ankle. Terrified and in agony, Krone summoned all of her strength to sit up. She looked up to see a horse coming straight at her.

The aptly named Two Is Trouble crushed Krone's left elbow and kicked her in the chest. "It hurt so bad, I remember thinking to myself, 'Pass out. Please pass out.' The only thing I wanted to be was unconscious."

Julie Krone climbed aboard Seattle Way on the final day of the summer racing season at Saratoga in 1993. It was a bright and beautiful day in the historic racing town in upstate New York, and Krone was fit and ready for another war on the track.

Julie Krone smiles after riding Dance to Fit to win at Lone Star Park in Grand Prairie, Texas, April 18, 1999. Krone, the winningest female jockey and the only one to ever take a Triple Crown race, rode three winners on her last day before retirement.

Krone spent three weeks in a hospital and underwent two operations as doctors rebuilt her shattered ankle with fourteen titanium screws and two steel plates. She was lucky to be alive, they said. Her heart had been bruised. Fortunately, she had been wearing a flak jacket. The doctor told her to forget about racing.

Krone didn't listen.

"Now, this was a woman who knew pain," said Robert Bazley, her physical therapist. "But she was more than willing to put herself through even more pain to get back riding."

Growing up in Eau Claire, Michigan, Krone fell in love with horses at an early age. A fearless two-year-old, she was already riding ponies. "Julie would try anything," said her father. "Every day was a missile launch."

Julie's mother, a professional equestrienne, taught her daughter everything she knew about horses. Later, she used her connections to get Julie work as a groom and exercise rider at Churchill Downs. Julie was only fifteen at the time, too young to be eligible for such work, but her mother had fixed her birth certificate so she would appear to be sixteen. That was in the spring of 1979.

One year later, she entered her first professional race at Tampa Bay Downs and, in 1981, she rode her first winner. Julie moved to racing-rich Florida with her mother, now divorced, and found a valuable mentor in former jockey Julie Snellings, who had been paralyzed in a race and now worked at the Tampa Bay track.

"Little Julie Krone bebopped into the office one day," Snellings recalled. "I thought she was some feisty kid whose daddy had let her put on his racing helmet."

Krone might have looked like a kid, but she reacted like a hardened veteran whenever male jockeys—or anyone else—tried to intimidate her. "People knew right away that if they tried to chase Julie, she'd tell them where to get off," Snellings recalled. Snellings not only introduced Krone to important people around the track, she advised her not to fly off the handle when provoked. But it just wasn't in Julie's nature to let it go unnoticed.

Several years later at Monmouth Park in New Jersey, Krone displayed her aggressive personality in dramatic fashion. She had just completed a lopsided victory when one of the male jockeys in the race pulled up beside her, cursed her, and slashed her in the face with his whip. Bleeding, she continued on to the winner's circle and waited until the awards ceremony was over before she sought revenge.

Krone found the jockey and punched him in the nose. He was so angry he pushed her into a swimming pool, holding her head underwater. Shaking herself free, Krone ended the brawl by slamming a lawn chair over his head. The male jockey was suspended and Krone was fined, but she had earned the respect of her peers.

Krone was horse racing's version of The Little Engine That Could. No one would have blamed her if she had bowed out after that horrible accident at Saratoga. But nine months later, Krone was back in the saddle. She retired in 1999 with a string of successes at major tracks second to few jockeys, men or women.

There were other fine women jockeys before Krone—Barbara Jo Rubin, Mary Bacon and Kathy Kusner, to name a few. Whoever follows will find Krone's standards extremely difficult to meet. As Georgina Frost, a young Englishwoman learning her craft with Krone's guidance, once observed: "Julie's not a trailblazer. The trail that she blazed closed behind her as quickly as she opened it."

In March of 2000, a year after retiring from horse racing, Julie Krone was nominated for induction to the National Thoroughbred Racing Hall of Fame.

"Julie would try anything," said her father. Growing up in Eau Claire, Michigan, Krone fell in love with horses at an early age. A fearless two-year-old, she was already riding ponies. "Every day was a missile launch.

After Krone won a lopsided victory, a male competitor pulled up beside her, cursed her, and slashed her in the face with his crop. When Krone later punched him in the nose, he pushed her into a swimming pool and held her head underwater. Once free, Krone slammed a lawn chair over his head, ending the brawl. The jockey was suspended and Krone fined, but she had earned the respect of her peers.

Susan Butcher ☆ **Idatarod Musher**

While Libby Riddles was the first female musher to win the famed Iditarod dog sled race, Butcher was the first to dominate it. She won from 1986-88 and again in 1990, an unprecedented streak to make the men jealous.

Although Butcher tended to downplay her victories by crediting the dogs rather than her ability as a driver, she proved in overwhelming fashion that a woman could handle the rigors of one of the world's most grueling sporting endeavors.

FIRST LADY
Gertrude Ederle ★ English Channel Swimmer

On her first attempt to swim the English Channel, Gertrude Ederle failed. On her second try, everything was against her—literally.

Ederle was determined to become the first woman to swim across the Channel, or die trying. The success rate for completing the twenty-one-mile journey from France to England's White Cliffs of Dover was low. In fact, only five men had mastered the treacherous Channel at that point, including Enrique Tirabocci, who had set the world record of 16 hours, 33 minutes in 1923.

Ederle, the broad-shouldered daughter of a New York butcher, was already recognized as one of the world's great swimmers when she took the Channel plunge in 1925 and again in 1926. She was a gold medal winner at the 1924 Olympics with twenty-nine world and national swimming records to her credit.

The odds were surely against her. The longest event in the Olympics for women was 400 meters, so it was thought that twenty-one miles was much too far for them to swim. But Ederle was no stranger to long-distance swims, having completed the previous year a twenty-one-mile race between Manhattan's docks and Sandy Hook, New Jersey, in seven hours.

Standing on the shore in Cape Gris-Nez, Ederle hoped to make history. She wore a two-piece black silk swimming suit with a small American flag sewn above one breast, a red rubber cap and goggles made of amber glass. At shortly after seven in the morning, she scanned the depressing gray skies, said "Cheerio!" and dove into the cold, dark water.

By afternoon, squalls battered Ederle this way and that, sweeping her off course as she struggled against the violent elements. The sea was so rough that people on the accompanying boats became sick.

Ederle was sick, too, but not too sick to continue.

Finally, 14 hours and 31 minutes later, the exhausted Ederle stumbled onto the English shore. Not only had she completed the treacherous journey, she had gone an estimated fourteen miles out of her way and broken a world record by two hours!

chapter ten

"*You* think about the Hall of Fame . . . you strive to get in when you first start playing," Nancy said. "It's a very special thing to see your name up there with Babe . . ."

Legends of the Links

*b*abe Didrikson could hold her own with Babe Ruth. Nancy Lopez could do the same with Arnold Palmer.

Few women have had the impact of a Didrikson or a Lopez in their sport. While Lopez always sought to make her name on the links, Didrikson found golf later in life.

Before that, she was simply the greatest female athlete on the planet. She won two gold medals and a silver at the 1932 Olympics and, had she been allowed to compete in more events, Didrikson certainly would have added to her collection.

Even today, nearly a half-century after her death, Babe is considered to be the best woman athlete in history.

Babe excelled at every sport she tried. Her most lasting fame would come from her Olympic experience and her performances on the fairways and greens, though there wasn't a pursuit—athletic or otherwise—that Babe couldn't conquer.

"I've always been taught that if you are going to compete, you should do it as well as you can," she said. "That means being in the best shape you can be and being ready to do everything you can to win."

So, from the time she was a kid, Babe succeeded in softball, basketball, swimming, diving, and volleyball. There was running, of course, which would provide her first route to fame and glory.

Babe was such a tomboy and so good in competition—and unafraid to mention it—that she had few friends in high school. When offered a spot on the Employers Casualty Company basketball team, Babe left Beaumont, Texas, to live, work, and play in Dallas.

In her first game for the Golden Cyclones, the team sponsored by the insurance company, Babe outscored the entire opposing squad. She would eventually lead the Cyclones to three national amateur titles.

But it was not in basketball that Babe would become a household name, it was on the track.

> "I've always been taught that if you are going to compete, you should do it as well as you can," Babe said. "That means being in the best shape you can be and being ready to do everything you can to win."

Mildred "Babe" Didrikson *(far right)* **came back with her second world record performance in the Summer Olympics of 1932. She won the first heat of the 80-meter hurdles in 11.8 seconds, breaking the Olympic record of 12.2**

Babe Didrikson Zaharias urges the ball into the cup on the 18th green of Chicago's Tam O' Shanter Country Club in the women's All-American Golf Tournament, August 4, 1950.

Competing for Employers Casualty, she single-handedly won dual meets. She won ninety-two medals in the 1930 and 1931 track and field seasons competing as a runner, jumper, and thrower.

And she hadn't even been to the Olympics! That opportunity would come in 1932 at Los Angeles, when Babe qualified by winning five of the eight events she entered. Once again, she had more points than any other team.

Asked how she would fare in LA against the world's best, Babe smiled and said, "I'm going to win the high jump and set a world record. I don't know who my opponents are, and it won't make any difference anyway."

While she managed only a silver medal in the high jump—she dove head-first over the bar, which infuriated officials who penalized her for lack of technique—Babe won the javelin throw and the 80-meter hurdles and was quickly proclaimed the best female athlete in the world.

Then, just as she was beginning to celebrate her victories, she was declared ineligible for having appeared in an automobile advertisement, though she claimed Chrysler used her photo without permission. She planned to fight the decision, which was later rescinded. Reconsidering this plan of action, Babe decided to take advantage of her new professional status by earning money through personal appearances and competing in various sports exhibitions.

But Babe needed a steady livelihood, so she opted for golf, a game at which she was anything but a natural.

Her hands bled from the hours of practice she needed just to become competitive in golf. But she shot a 95 in her first full round—without any knowledge of how to putt or play out of sand traps. Soon Babe was taking lessons and her scores dropped into the eighties.

By 1934, she felt ready for a tournament and entered the Fort Worth Invitational. Babe won her first match with a 77, then was eliminated.

But the sport had gotten her competitive juices flowing again. The following April she won the prestigious Texas Women's Amateur, then was promptly banned when competitors in the tournament, citing Didrikson's career as a professional in other sports, complained that she had not competed as an amateur.

At first, Babe performed in golf exhibitions, often against men. When she did play in the very few professional events that were available at the time, she did not

“ Pro golf was still a challenge,” Didrikson said. “I hoped by turning pro I would better women's golf by forcing more open tournaments.” Toward that end, Babe and her husband, promoter George Zaharias, helped found the LPGA. One year later, she was voted the best female athlete of the first half-century.

Babe Didrikson, top scorer in the qualifying round of the Helen Dohorty Women's Golf Tournament, on the first day of play in Miami on January 28, 1947. *(right)* She shot an 87, nine over par, during her first major tournament against men at the Southern California Open in Glendale, December 17, 1936. *(far right)*

collect prize money because she sought to reinstate her amateur status. Nonetheless, in 1940 she captured the Western Open and Texas Open, the only two women's professional tournaments.

In 1944, her amateur standing was reinstated by the U.S. Golf Association. She celebrated by winning nearly everything she entered, including the 1945 Western Open despite the death of her mother during the tournament.

The next year she began a winning streak that would reach an incredible seventeen tournaments before turning pro again—partly to accept a $300,000 offer to make a movie. Mostly, she turned pro because she sought the best competition.

"Pro golf was still a challenge," she said. "I hoped by turning pro I would better women's golf by forcing more open tournaments."

Toward that end, Babe and her husband, promoter George Zaharias, helped found the LPGA. One year later, she was voted the best female athlete of the first half-century.

In 1944, her amateur standing was reinstated by the U.S.G.A. She celebrated by winning nearly everything she entered, including the 1945 Western Open despite the death of her mother during the tournament. . . . The next year she began a winning streak that would reach an incredible seventeen tournaments before she turned pro again to compete against the best women athletes.

Other women, most notably Patty Berg, Louise Suggs, Betsy Rawls and Betty Jameson, played major roles in the establishment of the LPGA. Clearly, Babe was its star, and the association grew quickly from eight to thirty members. Membership continued to grow as more tournaments were added to the schedule.

Sadly, Babe would not live to see the LPGA become the institution it is today. In 1952, the day after winning a tournament in her hometown of Beaumont, she was diagnosed with cancer.

Amazingly, she returned to the tour after surgery and won another Women's Open. Just after her eighty-second career victory, at the Spartanburg Open, Babe collapsed. More cancer was discovered, and this time surgery was not an option.

Babe died on Sept. 27, 1956. She would know little or nothing of the great players who would follow her, from Kathy Whitworth and Mickey Wright to Joanne Carner and Carol Mann. She would never hear the name Nancy Lopez.

Anyone who possesses even a casual knowledge of women's golf in the last thirty years knows about Nancy Lopez. What Palmer did for the men's tour in the 1950s and 1960s—what Tiger Woods is doing for the sport of golf now—Lopez did for the women's game in the 1970s and 1980s.

Not only was Lopez a Hall of Fame-caliber player and a charismatic figure, as was Palmer, she was a savior. Until she rolled onto the LPGA tour in 1978—and right over the competition—women's golf was floundering, receiving little media attention, low television ratings and barely any advertising dollars.

Already a champion at every amateur level, Lopez finished second in the 1975 U.S. Women's Open while a senior in high school. With the men's tour brimming with superstars (Palmer, Jack Nicklaus, Lee Trevino, Tom Watson), the women needed a dominant personality, a player of paramount skill and charm. They found her in Lopez.

As a rookie, she won eight tournaments, five of them in a row. And she won with a smile, modest words, and incredible shots.

Lopez began playing golf almost daily at age seven and, by the time she was twelve, she was beating high school and college players. Lopez was taught the game of golf by her father, an auto body shop owner in Roswell, New Mexico. An insatiable reader, she would browse through instructional books and magazine articles on golf, retaining just about everything she read, then apply those lessons on the course.

As a member of the high school boys' team, she also learned quickly about dealing with pressure.

"That was not exactly the most comfortable arrangement," she said, "but when they saw I could play, they left me alone."

Lopez soon would leave all her competition behind as she rose quickly to the top of the leaderboard. But she was hardly alone, for fans flocked to watch her at every tournament she entered. Arnie's Army had nothing on Nancy's Navy. Other great players of the day—Pat Bradley, Patty Sheehan, Betsy King, Sandra Haynie and Carner—were just a few of the women on the tour who would benefit from the attention.

"It was important for our tour to have someone like Nancy," Carner said. "Of course, she could have let a few of us win once in a while. Nancy brought a spotlight to women's golf. We all got to share in that spotlight."

Despite distractions from a growing number of endorsement offers and the overwhelming size of her galleries, she won nine times in 1979. As in 1978, she was named Player of the Year and won the Vare Trophy for lowest scoring average.

Lopez was no flash in the pan. Throughout the 1980s and into the '90s she continued to be one of the most competitive women on the tour. She didn't win as often as she once did, partly because many of the young girls whom she inspired—young women like Dottie Pepper and Annika Sorenstam and Karrie Webb—wound up beating her on tour.

Also a homemaker with three children, Lopez dispelled any doubts that a mom could still be a competitive athlete. In fact, few sportswomen have done that as well as Lopez, who remains a top player even in her fourth decade on tour.

By century's end, she had won forty-eight LPGA titles and three majors. In honor of her achievement, Lopez was inducted into the LPGA Hall of Fame in 1987. The world's best amateur player is presented annually with the Nancy Lopez Award.

"You think about the Hall of Fame and you strive to get in when you first start playing on tour," she said. "It's a very special thing to see your name up there with a Babe Didrikson Zaharias."

"It was important for our tour to have someone like Nancy," Carner said. "Of course, she could have let a few of us win once in a while. Nancy brought a spotlight to women's golf. We all got to share in that spotlight.

chapter eleven

"We're good friends," said Martina Navratilova of Chris Evert, but things get a little touchy on both sides when we talk about our accomplishments.

Tennis Champions

She was talented and dangerous—and virtually unknown.

When Martina Navratilova stepped onto the tennis court in Akron, Ohio, in the spring of 1973, she was determined that her opponent, Chris Evert, would remember her name.

At eighteen, Evert was the rising star of women's tennis, having already beaten top-ranked Margaret Court in an exhibition match. Navratilova, a sixteen-year-old from Czechoslovakia, was in awe, yet Navratilova gave Evert one of the toughest matches of her young career while going down in defeat. At the end, Evert would have no choice but to remember her name.

Eventually, the competition between these two tennis players would become one of the greatest individual

The sixteen-year-old Chris Evert shows some of her winning form as she upset fifth seeded Francoise Durr of France during the women's third-round of the U.S. Open Tennis Championships at Forest Hills, N.Y., on September, 6, 1971. Evert received a standing ovation from the near capacity crowd of 12,500 as she swept the clinching game.

rivalries in the history of sports. For the better part of fifteen years, from 1973–1988, Navratilova and Evert competed against each other in matches that were often brutal tests of skill and endurance. Pushing each other to new heights of athletic achievement, they brought women's tennis into the spotlight. It was difficult to mention one without the other, they had become so inextricably linked.

Of course, there had been great women's tennis rivalries before theirs, most notably those of Helen Wills and Helen Jacobs, Billie Jean King and Margaret Court, as well as one between Chris Evert and Evonne Goolagong. Others, such as that between Monica Seles and Steffi Graf, would follow.

The Evert-Navratilova rivalry highlighted opposites both in temperament and style as it attracted new fans and sponsors to women's tennis. When

What young sports-minded woman didn't want to be like Evert, a pretty, ponytailed blonde, the quintessential "girl-next-door"? Or style their games after her? Girls all over America were practicing their two-handed backhands, just like Chris. And who didn't dream of being the next Navratilova, a state-of-the-art tennis player whose serve was the most deadly in the game? Like Martina, young women playing tennis were now into bodybuilding, daring to serve the ball across the court at a blazing ninety miles per hour.

Evert and Navratilova first competed against each other in 1973, total prize money for the women's tennis tour was $250,000. By 1990, it had increased to $23 million. Women's tennis had become big business, thanks in large part to Chris and Martina.

What young sports-minded woman didn't want to be like Evert, a pretty, ponytailed blonde, the quintessential "girl-next-door"? Or style her game after Evert? Girls all over America were practicing their two-handed backhands, just like Chris. And who didn't dream of being the next Navratilova, a state-of-the-art tennis player whose serve was the most deadly in the game? Like Martina, young women playing tennis were now into bodybuilding, daring to serve the ball across the court at a blazing ninety miles per hour.

A contest between Evert and Navratilova was an irresistible attraction. Their matches were often decided by which style was more effective on that day: Evert's brilliant, patient baseline game or Navratilova's aggressive rush-to-the-net approach, backed by the hardest serve in women's tennis.

It was the cool, composed Evert against the emotional, high-strung Navratilova. Billie Jean King once made the comment that "Martina is the best we've ever had, but she's not as good as Chris mentally. She lets her emotions get to her sometimes. Chris sustains the mental aspect of the game better than anyone."

Whereas other tennis rivalries may have been marked by bitterness and jealousy, the one between Evert and Navratilova grew into a friendship as they continued to battle each other on the court. It was a rivalry distinguished not only by great play but by good vibrations. "We're good friends, but things get a little touchy on both sides when we talk about our accomplishments," said Navratilova. "We know that if only one of us had been there, we would have won more. But," she concluded, "we would not have become as good a player."

> **"Martina is the best we've ever had, but she's not as good as Chris mentally," Billie Jean King once said. "She lets her emotions get to her sometimes. Chris sustains the mental aspect of the game better than anyone.**

Evert and Navratilova met eighty times, with thirty-three of their matches going the full three sets. Sixty of the matches were played in the finals of a tournament. Navratilova held a 43-37 edge overall, but until the latter years of their rivalry the number of wins was equal. When they retired from competition, these rivals ranked 1-2 in individual titles (167 for Navratilova and 157 for Evert) and 1-2 in matches won (1,405 for Navratilova and 1,309 for Evert). Navratilova was the all-time money winner among women until Graf surpassed her mark. Both earned over $20 million, while Evert made approximately $9 million.

Money and worldwide fame were just a dream for Navratilova until she defected to the United States. Though she had already been a national champion and a member of her country's Davis Cup team, she was unhappy with the way of life in Czechoslovakia. Now that the Russian occupation had become firmly entrenched, Navratilova felt that her country had lost its soul. She didn't believe she could reach her potential in tennis, either athletically or financially, in a Communist country.

The move to America was a gamble. Navratilova was barely nineteen when she left her family and friends to seek freedom in the United States. All of the hardships of expatriation awaited her when she arrived. At first, money was scarce. She struggled with the language. She felt awkward and different, very much a foreigner. She developed an appetite, however, for American fast foods. Hamburgers and pancakes became a daily staple—and a major problem. She would spend years fighting to keep down her weight.

"I remember her first win," said Ellen Merlo, who represented one of the sponsors on the women's tour. "All she wanted to do was to go to an IHOP and have pancakes and celebrate." Her career started to take off in 1975 when she won four tournaments. In 1978, she gained the No. 1 world

> **Despite all her victories, Navratilova did not have an easy time winning public acceptance. As quick with her temper as she was with a racket, Navratilova said what was on her mind—political correctness be damned.**

The title passes—Martina Navratilova (*right*) is congratulated at the net by Chris Evert after Martina won the women's singles title at the U.S. Open in New York, September, 10, 1983. Martina won the title for the first time by a score of 6-1, 6-3.

Martina stormed back from a disastrous first set to win 1-6, 6-4, 6-2 against Arantxa Sanchez Vicario in the quarter-finals

of the 1991 Virginia Slims Championships at New York's Madison Square Garden.

ranking, winning ten tournaments and taking home nearly $500,000 in earnings.

Then she went into a slump. Two long years were spent developing her game. A friend, Nancy Lieberman, came to the rescue. Lieberman, then one of the country's top basketball players, guided Navratilova through a severe training regimen which focused on diet as much as it did exercise. Pam Shriver, Navratilova's doubles partner, recalled that at the time Martina "didn't have the best working and nutritional habits."

In 1982, Navratilova came back to the women's tennis circuit with a vengeance. She was better—and more fit—than ever. And she had a monster year, winning ninety of ninety-three singles matches and fifteen of eighteen tournaments.

She took back the number one ranking and basically held it from 1982–1986. She was on top and so was the doubles team of Navratilova and Shriver, who did nothing but win in the '80s. At one point, they put together an amazing 109-match winning streak and eight straight Grand Slam titles.

Despite all her victories, Navratilova did not have an easy time winning public acceptance. As quick with her temper as she was with a racket, Navratilova said what was on her mind— political correctness be damned. Her outspoken ways and battles with the press often made headlines, occasionally resulting in lawsuits.

Chris Evert holds up her trophy after winning Wimbledon in 1974. She was voted 55th of the top 100 athletes of the century.

It would be difficult to think of Evert in a similar situation. Evert was more conscious of her public image and more gracious in defeat—at least while facing the cameras. Once, after a loss to Navratilova in the finals at Wimbledon, Evert warmly put her arm around her opponent and smiled as they posed for pictures. "If you hadn't seen the match, you would not have known who won," one writer said. Tennis great Rosie Casals observed, "Chris is more calculating, more conservative. She was brought up by a very conservative father. Chris has always tried to do the right thing."

Lucky for Evert that her father was a tennis teacher. She was only five when she first grabbed a racket, though tennis didn't interest her immediately.

"If my dad was a carpenter, I never would have played tennis," said Evert, a native of Fort Lauderdale, Florida. "I remember that when I was eight, I lost love-love to a girl from Miami Beach, and I came off the court smiling. I was thinking, 'This girl is older and better, so let's go to the mall.'"

That cavalier attitude vanished, however, once Evert started winning. And the transformation began quickly. "It gave me a sort of power, that I was able to do something well. That's a very strong feeling at a young age."

By the time Evert was fifteen, she made headlines with her victory over the great Margaret Court. At sixteen, Evert garnered further attention by making the semifinals at the U.S. Open. A year later, she was a semifinalist at Wimbledon and already a dominant force in women's tennis. She was also known as "The Ice Maiden" because of her emotionless style of play. Evert's court presence was something she had learned from her father. "I try to tell all my pupils not to get too excited out there," he said. "Emotions can be ammunition for the opponent."

"I'm seventeen years old and the whole world

Classmates welcome Chris back to school. At sixteen, Evert made headlines by playing in the semifinals at the 1971 U.S. Open. Though she was beaten by Billie Jean King a year later, she would become a semifinalist at Wimbledon and become a dominant force in women's tennis.

already knows me as Little Miss Icicle," Evert recalled of her 1972 appearance at Wimbledon. She was deeply hurt that the whole world saw her as being cold and uncaring when, in truth, she was just shy. She withdrew further within herself. "It wasn't until my late twenties that I was able to be more myself on the court."

Evert was America's sweetheart, but her innocent appearance belied her killer instincts on the tennis court. Quietly, almost politely, she would

> If my dad was a carpenter, I never would have played tennis," said Evert. "I remember that when I was eight, I lost love-love to a girl from Miami Beach, and I came off the court smiling. I was thinking, 'This girl is older and better, so let's go to the mall.'

put away opponents. In 1974, Evert set a modern record by winning fifty-four straight matches; in 1981 she won seventy-two of seventy-eight and smashed her way through Wimbledon without so much as losing a set. Soon the only suspense remaining was in how she would dispatch her opponents, whether through baseline brilliance or a chillingly consistent ground game.

Because Evert and Navratilova always seemed to be on a collision course to determine who was No. 1, it was only appropriate that one of their greatest matches took place at Wimbledon, the grand event of the tennis circuit. It was the fourth Wimbledon singles final for Evert, the first for Navratilova.

On the eve of the match, Navratilova lay doubled up in pain, writhing with cramps. She couldn't get out of bed, much less play against the top-ranked woman in the game. Tennis was the last thing on her mind. Evert, on the other hand, spent a pleasant day strolling around London with her future husband, John Lloyd. She was in much better shape for the finals, both mentally and physically.

That became apparent once the match began, as Evert easily beat Navratilova in the first set 6-2. Things didn't get any better for Navratilova in the second. She seemed distracted, completely missing the ball like an amateur while attempting to smash it across court. Later in the set, she was struck on the temple by one of Evert's hard volleys. Navratilova was embarrassed.

"You don't get hit very often, and certainly not in singles," she said. "But it woke me up. It set me on my way." The crowd came alive as Navratilova rallied, winning the second set 6-4. The upstart from Czechoslovakia had suddenly found her game. Then, just as the match was turning in her favor, it appeared that she would lose.

Evert took a 4-2 lead in the third set and was still up 5-4 when Navratilova won twelve of the last thirteen points to claim her first Wimbledon championship. Her comeback was so incredible that even *she* couldn't grasp her accomplishment. "I can't believe it," she said over and over again.

Six years would pass before Navratilova won against Evert consistently, but her stunning comeback at the 1978 Wimbledon championship set the tone for many more epic battles to come.

Evert set a modern record by winning fifty-four straight matches. In 1981 she won seventy-two of seventy-eight and smashed her way through Wimbledon without so much as losing a set.

As an International Tennis Hall of Fame inductee, Chris Evert (left) **returns a serve during her doubles match in the 1995 Virginia Slims Legends tournament. Evert and Olga Morozova defeated Billie Jean King and Rosie Casals 6-1.**

Six years would pass before Navratilova won against Evert consistently, but her stunning comeback at the 1978 Wimbledon championship set the tone for many more epic battles to come.

In 1984 Navratilova defeated Evert 6-3, 6-1 at the French Open in Roland Garros. The two pose at center court following their match in the Women's final. *(left)*

Althea Gibson ⭐

Tennis in the 1950s was a game reserved for whites. Althea Gibson changed all that.

"Some people have labeled me a pioneer," Arthur Ashe once said. "I am not a pioneer. I am following in the path that was blazed by Althea Gibson. If anyone deserves credit for being the model for our race and her gender, it is Althea Gibson. She fought the battles first, and she won those battles."

Growing up in a New York City ghetto, Gibson was a poor student with little use for school. She dropped out and, when she was fourteen, became a ward of the city.

During her time in welfare programs, she was introduced to a city game, paddleball, played against a wall with wooden rackets. Gibson was so adept at it that she tried other racket sports and quickly became a tennis prodigy.

Involvement in sports helped her mature, and soon she no longer had an attitude problem. She began winning tennis tournaments for minority players, catching the eye of several universities. Still, Gibson was barred from a majority of tennis clubs, which meant she couldn't prove herself against white players.

Then Alice Marble, a former Wimbledon champion, blasted the tennis community for its exclusion of blacks. Embarrassed, the U.S. tennis federation opened the sport to all amateurs. In 1952, Gibson ranked seventh nationally.

But she needed a breakthrough. It wouldn't come for five years, and Gibson often considered quitting.

Once she developed a balanced game, she soared to the top of her sport. Gibson won the singles and doubles competition at Wimbledon in 1957, then repeated the next year. She also won the singles crown at the U.S. Championships during that same period. She quickly became one of the most popular and recognizable female athletes in the world.

Then Gibson stunned everyone by quitting the game of tennis, citing an inability to make enough money to support herself.

Five years later, she was back in professional sports, this time as a player on the LPGA tour. As one would expect, Gibson broke racial barriers on the links with the same courage and perseverance she demonstrated on the tennis court.

Billie Jean King ✶

Had there been no Billie Jean King, women's sports would have still made the reforms she introduced. Eventually, women might have been compensated equally with men. They might have received equal opportunities in athletics. They might have known fame and fortune.

Because of Billie Jean King, they got it all—and more.

In 1961, she won the first of an unimaginable twenty Wimbledon titles by teaming with Karen Hantze for the doubles championship. King would win thirteen singles and doubles crowns at the U.S. Championships, six at the French Open, and three at the Australian.

Among her achievements off the court were co-founding the Women's Sports Foundation, organizing World Team Tennis, recruiting sponsors for the women's tennis tour she helped establish, and ensuring that women received increased purses until, finally, they would be on a par with the men.

But nothing she did had more impact than beating self-described "male chauvinist pig" Bobby Riggs in the most hyped tennis event ever.

Riggs was fifty-five, King twenty-nine. The match should have been a joke, one without an audience, but Riggs, with his entrepreneurial skills, turned it into an extravaganza.

He joked about the women's lib movement and criticized anyone who suggested that "the weaker sex" was not an accurate description of females, making the claim that he would beat every top woman tennis player once he finished off King.

If Riggs won, everything King wanted for women in sports might not have been possible. And she knew it.

King won 6-4, 6-3, 6-3 before 30,472 in the Houston Astrodome and a television audience of fifty million.

King used the attention to campaign for women's rights, gay rights (losing many of her endorsements after

admitting to lesbian relationships), and Title IX. She became a motivational speaker, a community leader, and, as always, a voice of reason in the sporting world.

"*t*here is a wide-open road for women's sports, particularly team sports," said Terry Taylor, Sports Editor of The Associated Press. "Little girls who watch things such as the Women's World Cup and the Final Four and the WNBA then say, 'I can do that, too . . . there's no stopping me.'"

Trail Blazers

American speed skater Bonnie Blair takes her victory lap with the Olympic mascots after winning the 1000-meter event in the 1994 Winter Olympics held in Hamar, Norway. This was Blair's fifth Olympic gold medal—more than any American woman has ever won. *(left)*

Bonnie Blair races in the women's 500-meter speed skating event during the 1994 Winter Olympics. Blair won her fourth career gold medal with a time of 39.25 seconds. *(overleaf)*

*i*t is virtually impossible—no, it is impossible—to profile every significant contributor to the development of women's sports.

And it is just as futile to rank them in any particular order.

But these women are pioneers. Each has played a major role in her sport or women's sports in general. Each deserves recognition.

★ SPEED SKATING

Bonnie Blair

There are few indisputable truisms in sports. Here's one: Bonnie Blair is the greatest American woman speed skater. She might be the top U.S. woman in any winter sport after capturing five gold medals in three Olympics.

Blair, whose family and friends would cheer her at major events with banners and T-shirts declaring themselves "The Blair Bunch," was born to the sport. She came into the world on March 18, 1964 while her older siblings were competing in a local event.

The youngest of six, Blair was winning state titles in Illinois when she was seven years old. By the age of sixteen, she was a world-class skater.

But competing on the speed skating circuit was problematic. In the early 1980s, there was little funding from the U.S. Olympic Committee or the speed skating federation, and virtually no money to be made from the sport. Sure, Eric Heiden was a hero at the 1980 Lake Placid Olympics with his five victories. Yet that had no effect on the structure or finances of speed skating.

Enter the Champaign, Illinois, police department, which raised money for Blair to train with the U.S. men's team and compete internationally. She made the 1984 Olympic squad and, by 1988, was by far the best female sprinter in the sport.

The investment paid off. For the rest of her career, the ice was gilded with gold for Bonnie Blair.

☆ TRACK & FIELD/MARATHON

Joan Benoit Samuelson

The bullheaded thinking that defined the International Olympic Committee for decades was exemplified by its refusal to allow women to run a marathon in the Games. Too fragile, the IOC said. Too long a distance. Too dangerous.

That was too much for Joan Benoit Samuelson to take. She might have stood only 5-foot-3 and weighed 100 pounds or so, but she filled a global spotlight at the 1984 Los Angeles Games.

Three months before the Olympics and a mere seventeen days before the U.S. team trials, she underwent arthroscopic surgery on her right knee. Everyone, even her coaches, told her it was over. . . . Not only did she run in the trials, she won them. Benoit Samuelson ran—and won—a marathon less than three weeks after surgery. . . .She takes a victory lap at the 1984 Olympics. *(above)*

Finally, a women's marathon was approved. And Benoit Samuelson was one of the favorites. Then, three months before the Olympics and a mere seventeen days before the U.S. team trials, she underwent arthroscopic surgery on her right knee.

Everyone, even her coaches, told her it was over.

No, it was not, she replied. Not only did she run in the trials, she won them. Joan Benoit Samuelson ran—and won—a marathon less than three weeks after surgery.

That made her runaway Olympic victory almost expected. Her display of determination and perseverance made the IOC's previous stance look foolish and antiquated.

Grete Waitz

Grete Waitz was a trendsetter in women's long distance running, once holding world marks in six events. She was the 1977 World Cup champion at 3,000 meters and a member of the 1972 and 1976 Norwegian Olympic teams at 1,500 meters. Waitz set world records for the 3,000 in 1975 and 1976, and was unbeaten in cross country races for twelve years, winning five world titles (1978-1981 and 1983).

When she switched to the marathon, Waitz was just as dominant, particularly in the New York City Marathon, which she won nine times. The first woman to run under 2 hours, 30 minutes for a marathon, Waitz was, along with Frank Shorter and Bill Rogers, responsible in great part for the flourishing of long distance running in the 1970s. She also organized an annual 5K race in Norway that draws nearly 45,000 women.

Waitz's success in the marathon encouraged other women to move from the track and try the longer event. By the 1990s it was common to see women compete at several distances throughout the track and road racing seasons, much as the men had done for decades.

Norway's Grete Waitz *(left)* **triumphantly crosses the finish line at the 1984 Summer Olympics to take the silver medal in the women's marathon. The first woman to run under 2 hours, 30 minutes for a marathon, Waitz was, along with Frank Shorter and Bill Rogers, responsible in great part for the flourishing of long distance running in the 1970s.**

Helen Wills Moody

Because she wore makeup during her matches in the Roaring Twenties, Wills was known as "Queen Helen." The nickname came mainly from her surpassing court play as she won nineteen major singles crowns, including seven U.S. Championships and an Olympics.

In an era that saw the likes of Babe Ruth, Red Grange and Jack Dempsey, Wills was the female equivalent. She brought unparalleled attention to women in her sport—and sports in general. Her rivalry with Helen Jacobs equaled that of Jack Dempsey and Gene Tunney or, in later days, Chris Evert and Martina Navratilova.

★ SWIMMING

Dawn Fraser

The Australian swimmer took gold medals in three straight Olympics: the 100 freestyle in 1956, 1960, and 1964. She was twenty-seven at the Tokyo Games, considered old for the sport, but she held off a slew of teenagers after overcoming tragedy and serious injury to win the gold.

Just seven months before the 1964 Olympics, Fraser broke her neck in an auto accident that killed her mother and seriously injured her sister. Doctors told her to forget about swimming—ever.

"That wouldn't be," she said. "I owed it to the memory of my mother to make it back."

And to get another gold medal.

Helen Wills Moody, who won eight Wimbledon titles and was one of

the premier figures in America's golden era of sports in the 1920s and '30s,

brought unparalleled attention to women in her sport—and to sports in general.

Australian Olympic champion Dawn Fraser sits on the edge of the pool in Houston, Texas, and towels off after breaking the American

record for the second time that day, winning the 110-yard freestyle event in the National AAU Senior women's outdoor swimming and

diving championships. The nineteen-year old champ's final record time was 1:03.9.

Donna de Varona at the Sydney 2000 Olympic site in 1999. *(above)*

Donna as a seventeen-year old high school girl *(left)* **displays the gold medal she won in 1964 after winning the women's 400-meter individual medley swim event at the Tokyo Olympics. She won the event with an Olympic record time of 5:18.7.**

Donna de Varona

No one has done more for the cause of women's sports in the last twenty years than de Varona.

An Olympian at thirteen, she won a pair of golds four years later in the 1964 Games. She held eighteen world records when she retired the next year at the tender age of eighteen.

From there, de Varona compiled a resume worthy of a Renaissance Woman:

★ The first female sportscaster on national television.
★ Co-founder of the Women's Sports Foundation.
★ Lobbyist for women's rights in sports, particularly the enforcement of Title IX.
★ Member of the President's Commission on Olympic Sports.
★ Chairperson of the 1999 Women's World Cup.

"I grew up as a child of the '60s and fought the battles," she said.

Most often, she won them.

Terry Taylor

Since 1992, the most powerful job in sports journalism has belonged to a woman.

Terry Taylor ascended to the Sports Editor position at The Associated Press just as women's sports began to flourish. She has seen the transformation first-hand while overseeing coverage of the biggest sporting events for the world's largest news organization.

"There is a wide-open road for women's sports, particularly team sports," Taylor said. "Little girls who watch things such as the Women's World Cup and the Final Four and the WNBA then say, 'I can do that, too, and I want to do that. There's no stopping me.'"

One of the keys to the surge in popularity for women's sports has been exposure. For years, television ignored just about anything involving women except figure skating, gymnastics, tennis and golf.

"And with gymnastics, it was every four years at the Olympics," Taylor noted. "Now there is more showcasing of women's sports, whether it's the Olympics or World Cups or other tournaments.

"Twenty years ago, do you think the Women's World Cup would sell out or be so magnificent?"

The way the media have covered women's sports has also changed drastically. So have the people doing the reporting.

"We have magazines now that concentrate on women's sports," observed Taylor. "You can start a professional soccer league and know it will get significant coverage. Maybe it's not stupid to think of a women's softball league, because we [in journalism] will pay attention."

Taylor said there is more of an awareness for women in journalism.

"Both students and sports editors say to me that women have been emboldened now. You do not see the same percentage of men. Gradually, women are covering all major sports—it used to be just hockey and tennis and figure skating. It's opened the way for more women's coverage.

"Years ago, if I saw another woman in the press box, it was, 'There's a buddy, there's another me out there.' Now, we are everywhere. We don't stick out and that's when you know we've arrived."

Phoenix Mercury coach Cheryl Miller, who has also coached on the college levels and worked as a television commentator, brought a hip, funky attitude to the women's game. It was just what the sport needed. Cheryl Miller signals to her players during a game. *(below)*

Ann Meyers

The first great women's college player, Meyers was to the UCLA Lady Bruins what Lew Alcindor or Bill Walton were to the men's team. She even had a three-day tryout with the Indiana Pacers, a publicity stunt, for sure, but it brought further attention to how well women could play basketball.

Meyers' dominant play and her popularity raised not only the school's program to a new level but the entire sport as well. Television became interested in the women's game when it realized how attractive women's basketball could be when played at the college level.

A longtime basketball sportscaster, she married Hall of Fame pitcher Don Drysdale, who died in 1993.

Cheryl Miller

Whereas Meyers provided a focal point for women's basketball, Miller was its flashpoint. She brought the playground to the college arena with her spins, ballhandling, jumping, and drives to the basket. Miller was the first woman to play the game above the rim.

Even as Miller was lifting women's basketball so high, women in college programs were still playing the six-on-six game in which three players stood at each end of the court, with no fast breaks and virtually no interaction.

Miller would have none of that. Her interaction was with the crowd—much as her younger brother Reggie has done in his NBA career. She took the game from the court to the people.

A four-time All-American at Southern Cal, where she won two NCAA titles, Miller led the 1984 United States team to the Olympic gold medal. Until then, America rarely contended for such honors.

Miller, who has also coached on the college and pro levels and worked as a television commentator, brought a hip, funky attitude to the women's game. It was just what the sport needed.

Nancy Lieberman-Cline

On the streets of Far Rockaway, New York, she was too good for all comers, men or women. She made the national team for the Pan American Games when she was in high school, then moved onto the Olympic squad the next year. Old Dominion won two college crowns with her in the backcourt. If there was a trophy available in women's sports, she won it.

Lieberman-Cline was the Pistol Pete Maravich of the women's game. She was so entertaining that the Harlem Globetrotters hired her to play for their opponent, the Washington Generals. Lieberman-Cline was so good that she played in the USBL, a men's pro league, in 1986.

At thirty-eight, she came out of retirement to play in the WNBA, where she also coached and served as the chief of basketball operations for the Detroit team.

In 1998, Lieberman-Cline was elected president of the Women's Sports Foundation.

"The next five years are very important to us in our growth, our acceptance and shaping where we're going to be as we head into the new millennium," she said in late 1999. "Athletics is going to be a fabric of everything we do."

Detroit Shock head coach Nancy Lieberman-Cline celebrates during the final moments of her squad's 82-68 win over the New York Liberty at the Palace of Auburn Hills, Michigan, in 1998. Lieberman-Cline led the Shock to a 17-13 record in its first season in the WNBA. *(bottom right)*

" The next five years are very important to us in our growth, our acceptance and shaping where

we're going to be as we head into the new millennium," said Nancy Lieberman-Cline, president of

the Women's Sports Foundation. "Athletics is going to be a fabric of everything we do. "

Nancy Lieberman-Cline of the WNBA's Phoenix Mercury poses after practice at America West Arena

in Phoenix in 1997. She waited sixteen years for the NBA to back a women's pro basketball league.

Donna Lopiano

As a child, Lopiano would make dents in a wall behind her house, throwing a baseball against it every day. By the time she was ready for Little League, she had the best arm in town. She planned on being the first woman in the major leagues.

But it was a girl's arm, and when she went to try out for the local Little League team, Lopiano was told to go home. Girls were not allowed.

That bitter lesson was never lost on her.

"I wasn't allowed to pursue my dream," she said, "and I believe everything I've done in my life has stemmed from that rejection."

In the early 1960s, the only place for such a talented female player to turn was the softball field. Lopiano's parents secured a tryout with the Raybestos Brakettes in nearby Stratford, Connecticut. And Lopiano easily made the roster on the best women's fast-pitch team.

She played nine seasons for the Brakettes, winning six national championships and three MVP awards, which secured her place in the National Softball Hall of Fame.

Then she turned her attention to equality in sports for women.

Having completed her master's and doctorate degrees in physical education, Lopiano coached three sports at Brooklyn College before being hired as athletic director for women at the University of Texas.

While sports were as male-dominated at Texas as at any university, Lopiano, backed by the Title IX legislation, set her goals high. Soon the Lady Longhorns were as formidable as any school, regularly winning conference and national championships. Lopiano's budget increased from $57,000 to $4 million a year. And more than 90 percent of the female athletes graduated, a number the Texas men—and the male athletes at most other schools—couldn't come close to matching.

But there was much more to do. In 1992, she left Texas to take charge of the Women's Sports Foundation. For the rest of the decade, Lopiano campaigned vigorously for women's rights in sports.

What she saw as the century ended was fulfilling, if not exactly perfect.

"It's like night and day," she said. "When I was playing, they were still wearing field hockey kilts to play basketball. The ball would get caught in your skirts. There's absolutely no comparison."

Lopiano's work is one reason why.

Donna Lopiano (*right*) speaks during a news conference in 1992 as newly named executive director of the Women's Sports Foundation with race car driver Lynn St. James, president of the foundation at the time. (*above*)

The foundation has been influential in furthering equality between men's and women's sports. It is involved in everything from fundraising, local-level development, and providing grants and scholarships to lobbying for political action. So pervasive is the WSF's influence that it has won the support of every major league and association in sports.

In February 2000, the International Olympic Committee honored the WSF, presenting it with the prestigious Women and Sport trophy, given to organizations and individuals who have made outstanding contributions to develop, encourage, and strengthen the participation of women and girls in sports.

USOC President William Hybl nominated the WSF for the award.

"The foundation has proven time after time that it is at the forefront of issues related to women in sport and America's athletes. We share with the Foundation that same commitment, and we are thrilled that the IOC has recognized the organization for its accomplishments," Hybl said.

"I feel the foundation has always been on the leading edge of the whole gender equity movement," executive director Donna Lopiano said. "Whenever the press has wanted perspective or comment, it's had the opportunity to create a self-fulfilling policy: to refute a myth or barrier. That has been tremendous positioning for changing the world."

The Women's Sports Foundation

Just the roll call of executives at the WSF, which was founded by Billie Jean King and Donna de Varona in 1974 to aid in supporting, publicizing, and representing women's athletics, is impressive. The membership is even more so, including everyone from Olympians to grass-roots coaches.

"This is a great time to be a female athlete, because we are getting so much recognition," said figure skater Michelle Kwan.

"For a young girl who wants to be in sports, there are so many opportunities . . .

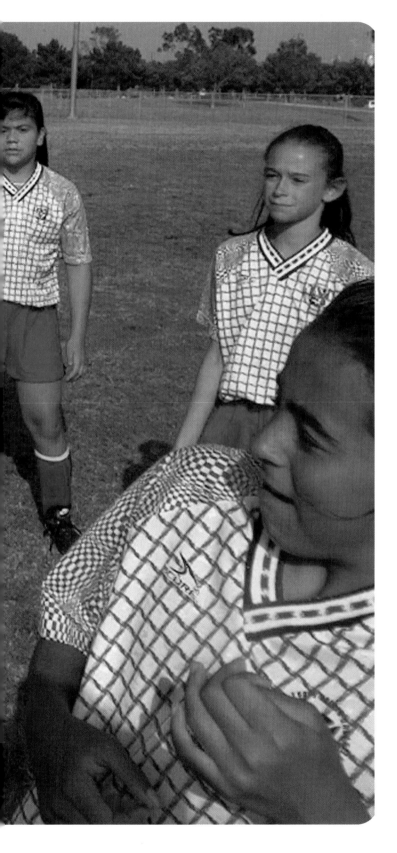

Houston Comets WNBA star Sheryl Swoopes *(right)* **greets members of the Englewood High girls basketball team.**

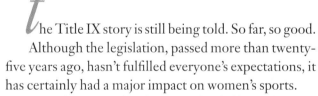he Title IX story is still being told. So far, so good.

Although the legislation, passed more than twenty-five years ago, hasn't fulfilled everyone's expectations, it has certainly had a major impact on women's sports.

Now, because of Title IX, girls of all ages have an opportunity to compete in sports that were once restricted to them, with role models like Mia Hamm, Cammi Granato, and Sheryl Swoopes leading the way. From the grass-roots level to professional leagues, a golden age for women's athletics has only just begun.

"This is a great time to be a female athlete, because we are getting so much recognition and women's sports have become so popular," said figure skater Michelle Kwan. "For a young girl who wants to be in sports, there are so many opportunities, and they are taking advantage of them."

ACKNOWLEDGMENTS

*The authors would like to acknowledge the help of the following people in
the researching and writing of this book:*

Nancy Armour

Frank Carroll

Doug Ferguson

Richard Finn

Shep Goldberg

Beth Harris

Aaron Heifetz

Heather Linhart

Marie Millikan

Tip Nunn

Lynn Plage

Bert Rosenthal

Gloria Cordes Elliott

Mickey Childress

George Mitterwald

Jennifer Gillom

Orwell Moore

Donna Lopiano

ABOUT THE AUTHORS

Ken Rappoport covered every major sport
during his thirty-year career as a writer for The Associated Press.
An award-winning freelance writer, Ken has written over twenty-five books for
both adults and young readers, including biographies of Nolan Ryan, Grant Hill,
Shaquille O'Neal and Wayne Gretzky.

Barry Wilner has been a sportswriter for the Associated Press since 1976.
He has covered some of the world's largest sporting events,
including fifteen Superbowls, six Stanley Cups, four World Cups,
and seven Olympic Games.

Rappoport and Wilner's first book, *They Changed the Game*,
a chronicle of sports pioneers in the 20th century, was published by
Andrews McMeel in the fall of 1999.